The Art of Conversation

The Art of Conversation:

How to Talk with Anyone about Anything in a Deep and Meaningful Way

RIKROSES
BOOKS AND E-BOOKS

SUMMARY

INTRODUCTION

Imagine effortlessly engaging in conversations that flow with the ease of a well-rehearsed dance. No longer do you face the awkwardness of forced silences or the anxiety of finding the right things to say. Instead, you find yourself immersed in genuine connection, exchanging ideas with passion, and uncovering the hidden depths of human experience. This, my friend, is the magic of mastering the art of conversation.

For many, the art of conversation is shrouded in mystery. It's a skill seemingly reserved for the extroverts, the social butterflies who flit from interaction to interaction with effortless charm. However, the truth is, the art of conversation is a learnable skill, accessible to anyone willing to embark on the journey of self-discovery and mindful communication.

This book is your guide on this transformative journey. Within its pages, you'll discover the secrets to unlocking your inner conversationalist, learning to navigate the intricate dance of words and emotions that forms the very foundation of connection. We'll explore the power of active listening and open-ended questions, unveiling the art of storytelling and navigating the complexities of difficult topics. You'll learn to overcome shyness and social anxiety, building confidence and rapport with ease.

But this book goes beyond mere techniques and strategies. It delves into the heart of human interaction, exploring the importance of empathy, respect, and genuine curiosity. We'll discover how the art of conversation transcends small talk, becoming a powerful tool for building meaningful relationships, fostering personal growth, and enriching your life in ways you never imagined.

Whether you're a seasoned professional seeking to elevate your communication skills, or an individual yearning for deeper connections, this book is your invitation to step into the world of transformative conversation. Here, you'll find the tools and insights needed to unlock your voice, embrace the power of listening, and embark on a remarkable journey towards becoming a master of the art of connection.

So, let us begin. Open your mind, prepare your heart, and embark on the path towards becoming the conversationalist you've always dreamed of being. The world awaits your voice, and the power of connection is yours to discover.

6

CHAPTER 1: Finding Your Voice

In the grand orchestra of human interaction, conversation plays the lead role. It is the delicate instrument that bridges the gap between individual hearts, ignites the flame of understanding, and propels relationships forward. Yet, for many, this seemingly simple act of exchanging words feels like a locked door, barring entry to a hidden world of connection and intimacy.

But the key to unlocking this door lies not in brute force, but in a more subtle, introspective journey – the journey of finding your voice. This voice is the unique blend of your experiences, perspectives, and emotions, the melody that resonates within you, waiting to be shared with the world.

Unveiling the Tapestry of Your Being:

This journey of self-discovery begins with a deep dive into the wellspring of your being. Imagine yourself standing in front of a vast, illuminated tapestry, woven with the threads of your life. As you gaze upon it, ask yourself these questions:

- ✓ What ignites your passion? What are those activities, topics, or ideas that make your eyes sparkle and your heart sing?
- ✓ What are your guiding stars? What principles and values inform your decisions and shape your interactions with the world?
- ✓ What stories does your tapestry tell? From the triumphs and joys to the trials and tribulations, every experience has contributed to the unique pattern of your being.

As you delve into these questions, allow the answers to surface from the depths of your soul. They are the threads that weave the fabric of your individuality, the foundation upon which your voice will be built.

7

Crafting Your Unique Instrument:

Once you have identified the essence of your being, the next step is to carefully craft your individual instrument of expression. Imagine this instrument as a finely crafted violin, waiting for your touch to bring forth its unique melody. Consider these practices as you refine its sound:

- ✓ **Become a lifelong student:** Immerse yourself in knowledge by reading diverse books, engaging in stimulating discussions with individuals from different backgrounds, and exploring new and challenging perspectives. The more you learn, the richer and more resonant your voice will become.

- ✓ **Develop your own opinions:** Don't be afraid to stand up and challenge the status quo. Embrace healthy dissent, form your own well-reasoned opinions, and express them with confidence. Remember, your unique perspective has the power to enrich and expand conversations.

- ✓ **Refine your communication skills:** Practice expressing yourself clearly, concisely, and authentically. This includes honing your active listening skills, developing your emotional intelligence, and mastering the art of non-verbal communication.

Becoming a Master of Your Melody:

Now that your instrument is ready, it's time to step onto the stage and share your unique melody with the world. Here are ways to liberate your voice and engage in meaningful connections:

- ✓ **Seek out diverse conversations:** Actively engage with individuals from different walks of life. Whether it's a lively discussion with your neighbor, a stimulating conversation with a colleague from another department, or an impromptu chat with a stranger on a train journey, each interaction offers an opportunity to expand your understanding of the world and enrich your own voice.

- ✓ **Contribute to dialogues:** Don't be a passive observer in conversations. Share your insights, challenge assumptions, and offer your unique perspective. Remember, your voice has the power to spark meaningful change, broaden perspectives, and foster deeper connections.

8

✓ **Express yourself creatively:** Writing, storytelling, music, and other creative pursuits can be powerful tools for self-discovery and communication. Use them to explore the depths of your inner world, process your experiences, and share your unique perspective with others in new and engaging ways.

Embrace the Journey of Growth:

Remember, finding your voice is not a destination, but a lifelong journey of evolution and refinement. As you navigate this path, there will be stumbles, moments of self-doubt, and occasional detours. Embrace these imperfections as stepping stones on your journey, learning from each experience and allowing them to shape your voice in new and unexpected ways.

Here are some reminders to guide you through the inevitable challenges:

✓ **Celebrate your uniqueness:** Don't fall into the trap of comparing your voice to others. Every individual possesses a unique melody, and yours is just as valuable and deserving of being heard.

✓ **Focus on progress, not perfection:** Be kind to yourself and remember that progress, not perfection, is the key to growth. Every conversation, every interaction, is an opportunity to learn and evolve. Embrace the journey and enjoy the process of becoming a more confident and articulate communicator.

✓ **Practice, practice, practice:** The more you speak up and share your voice, the more comfortable and confident you will become. Don't let the fear of imperfection paralyze you. Embrace opportunities to practice your communication skills in different settings and with diverse individuals.

A Continuous Symphony of Connection:

As you embark on this continuous journey of finding your voice, remember that it is not a solitary pursuit. You are not merely a solo musician playing in a vacuum, but rather a vital member of a grand orchestra of human connection. Your voice, when blended with the voices of others, creates a harmonious symphony that enriches the world around you.

9

Embrace the opportunity to learn from the voices of others. Listen actively, engage in thoughtful dialogue, and allow yourself to be inspired by the unique perspectives and experiences that others share. Remember, every voice has something valuable to offer, and by opening yourself to the music of others, you broaden your own understanding of the world and enrich your own melody.

More importantly, use your voice to build bridges of connection and understanding. In a world often characterized by division and conflict, your voice can be a powerful instrument for fostering empathy, compassion, and collaboration. Speak up for what you believe in, advocate for those who cannot speak for themselves, and use your voice to create a more just and equitable world.

Finding your voice is not about achieving perfection or becoming the most eloquent speaker in the room. It is about embracing your authenticity, sharing your unique perspective with the world, and using your voice to connect with others and make a positive impact on the world around you. So, take a deep breath, find your courage, and let your voice be heard. The world needs your melody.

As you continue refining your voice and sharing it with the world, remember that it is a delicate instrument, requiring both care and courage. Just as a skilled musician takes time to tune their instrument and build their confidence, so too must you nurture your voice and navigate the inevitable challenges that arise.

Overcoming the Blaring Static:

In the vast orchestra of human interaction, there will be moments when your voice feels drowned out by the cacophony of others. It might be the imposing figure in a meeting who monopolizes the conversation, the barrage of social media notifications, or the internal anxieties that make you hesitate to speak your truth.

Here are some strategies to help your voice rise above the static:

- ✓ **Embrace assertive communication:** Be clear, concise, and direct in expressing your thoughts and opinions. Don't shy away from asserting your needs and desires while remaining respectful of others.

- ✓ **Develop your listening skills:** Become an active listener, giving others your full attention and acknowledging their perspectives. This fosters trust and creates space for your voice to be heard in return.

10

✓ **Manage self-doubt:** Recognize and challenge negative self-talk that holds you back. Instead, focus on your strengths and accomplishments, and remind yourself that your voice is valuable and deserving to be heard.

Playing with Harmony and Dissonance:

Not every interaction will be a harmonious duet. There will be moments when your voice clashes with others, sparking disagreements and challenging conversations. These moments, however, are vital opportunities for growth and understanding.

✓ **Embrace healthy conflict:** View disagreements not as obstacles but as opportunities for deeper dialogue and learning. Listen with an open mind to opposing viewpoints and strive to find common ground, even if partial agreement is all that's achieved.

✓ **Develop your emotional intelligence:** Learn to manage your emotions effectively, especially in challenging situations. This allows you to express yourself assertively and respectfully, even when you disagree.

✓ **Seek common ground:** Even in the midst of disagreement, focus on finding areas of shared values or experiences. This can create a foundation for understanding and foster constructive dialogue.

The Melody of a Lifetime:

As you navigate the ebbs and flows of conversation, remember that finding your voice is a lifelong journey, not a destination. Embrace the continuous learning, the unexpected detours, and the moments of self-discovery that shape your unique melody.

✓ **Celebrate your evolution:** Acknowledge and celebrate the progress you make, both in your communication skills and in your understanding of yourself and the world around you.

✓ **Embrace humility:** Remain open to learning and evolving. Be willing to adapt your perspectives and refine your voice as you gain new knowledge and experience.

11

✓ **Enjoy the journey:** Above all, find enjoyment in the process of self-expression and connection. Let your voice be a source of joy, creativity, and purpose in your life.

Conclusion

By embracing your voice and sharing it with the world, you become a powerful instrument for change. You contribute to the beautiful symphony of human connection, weaving together individual melodies into a tapestry of understanding, empathy, and shared humanity. So, pick up your unique instrument, find your rhythm, and let your voice soar. The world is waiting to hear your melody.

CHAPTER 2: Becoming a Good Listener

While many believe conversation thrives on the eloquent speaker, the true magic lies in the art of listening. Imagine the greatest dancer frozen mid-step, unable to respond to their partner's movements. A conversation flourishes when both speaker and listener engage in a dynamic dance, a give-and-take where each role holds equal importance.

Active listening, the cornerstone of meaningful connection, transcends simply hearing words. It's about diving into the deeper layers, understanding the emotions woven between the lines, and grasping the unspoken thoughts that dance beneath the surface.

Active Listening: A Deeper Dive

Imagine a sculptor painstakingly chiseling away at a block of marble, revealing the hidden beauty within. Active listening is similar. We chip away at the surface of words, patiently uncovering the emotions, intentions, and meaning that lie beneath. It's a multi-faceted skill, encompassing:

- ✓ **Full Attention:** Imagine a friend pouring their heart out, only to see you scrolling through your phone. Distractions are conversation killers. Turn off your devices, face the speaker, and maintain eye contact – not a fixated stare, but a warm, inviting gaze that conveys your full engagement. A fidgeting foot or a wandering eye speaks louder than words, so be mindful of your nonverbal cues.

- ✓ **Open-mindedness:** Picture a world where everyone has the same opinion. Dull, right? Approach conversations with an open mind, free from preconceived notions and judgments. Embrace diverse perspectives, even

13

when they challenge your own. Set aside your need to control the conversation or impose your agenda. Remember, the goal is to explore, not to dominate.

✓ **Empathy:** Imagine yourself standing in a raging storm, feeling lost and alone. Wouldn't you appreciate someone who understood your pain and offered a warm embrace? In conversation, practice empathy. See the world through the speaker's eyes, feel their emotions, and reflect them back through verbal and nonverbal cues. A nod, a thoughtful "hmm," or even mirroring their facial expressions can create a bridge of understanding.

✓ **Insightful Questions:** Imagine a child asking endless questions, eager to learn and understand. Open-ended questions are your magic wand in conversation. Instead of questions answered with a simple "yes" or "no," delve deeper. Ask "why," "how," and "what else" to encourage elaboration and uncover hidden depths. Follow-up questions demonstrate genuine interest and ensure you're truly walking in the speaker's shoes.

✓ **Golden Silence:** Imagine two musicians playing competing melodies, creating disharmony instead of a beautiful symphony. Silence can be just as powerful as speech in conversation. Don't feel obligated to fill every pause with words. Give the speaker space to gather their thoughts, reflect, and even bask in the comfortable silence. Sometimes, the most meaningful communication transcends words.

Unlocking the Benefits

Active listening isn't just a conversational skill; it's a life tool. By honing this skill, you can:

✓ **Build deeper connections:** Imagine forging friendships where you truly see and understand each other. Active listening fosters genuine connections, creating a safe space for vulnerability and trust.

✓ **Resolve conflicts effectively:** Imagine a heated argument where both parties listen and truly understand each other's perspectives. Active listening allows you to de-escalate conflict, find common ground, and reach solutions that work for everyone.

14

✓ **Gain valuable insights:** Imagine a world where everyone shares their unique experiences and knowledge. Active listening opens doors to new perspectives, broadens your understanding of the world, and helps you learn and grow.

✓ **Become a more impactful communicator:** Imagine your words carrying weight and meaning. Active listening helps you tailor your communication to resonate with your audience, making you a more impactful speaker and influencer.

✓ **Discover hidden truths:** Imagine uncovering the true essence of a person or situation. Active listening allows you to see beyond the surface, uncover hidden emotions and intentions, and discover the beauty that lies beneath.

Mastering the Art: Practice Makes Perfect

Remember, becoming a good listener is a continuous journey, not a destination. Be patient with yourself, embrace the learning process, and celebrate your progress. Here are some exercises to help you refine your active listening skills:

✓ **Repeat and Reflect:** Imagine a mirror reflecting back your image. Practice reflecting the speaker's words back to them, ensuring you understand their message and inviting them to elaborate.

✓ **Paraphrase and Clarify:** Imagine a translator bridging the gap between different languages. Paraphrase the speaker's statements, demonstrating your understanding and creating space for further discussion.

✓ **Ask the Right Questions:** Imagine a detective piecing together clues to solve a mystery. Frame insightful questions that draw out the speaker's thoughts and emotions, guiding them to reveal their true message.

✓ **Embrace Nonverbal Communication:** Imagine a silent language spoken through gestures and expressions. Be mindful of your body language and facial expressions, ensuring they complement your verbal cues and convey genuine interest and understanding.

✓ **Step Outside Your Comfort Zone:** Imagine venturing into uncharted territory. Practice having conversations with people from diverse

15

backgrounds and perspectives. This will challenge your assumptions, broaden your understanding, and enrich your listening skills.

Conclusion

Remember, active listening is a gift you give to yourself and others. By mastering this art, you'll unlock the true power of conversation, paving the way for deeper connections, meaningful understanding, and a richer, more fulfilling life.

16

CHAPTER 3: The Power of Open-Ended Questions

Imagine a conversation as a journey. Closed-ended questions are like stepping stones, leading you from one point to the next in a predictable and linear fashion. They offer limited insight, revealing only the bare minimum of information. Open-ended questions, on the other hand, are like sprawling landscapes, inviting you to explore hidden depths and discover unexpected treasures. They unlock the doors to genuine connection, fostering deeper understanding and meaningful interaction.

What are open-ended questions?

Open-ended questions are those that cannot be answered with a simple "yes" or "no." Instead, they encourage the other person to elaborate, share their thoughts and feelings, and provide detailed responses. These questions are often phrased using words like "how," "why," "what," "tell me more," or "could you explain?"

Why are they so powerful?

The power of open-ended questions lies in their ability to:

- ✓ **Shift the conversation from information exchange to exploration:** Instead of simply gathering facts, open-ended questions pave the way for meaningful dialogue. They encourage participants to think critically, delve into their own perspectives, and share their unique experiences.

- ✓ **Unveil hidden depths:** Unlike closed-ended questions which scratch the surface, open-ended questions allow you to uncover the other person's

17

values, beliefs, motivations, and personal narratives. This deeper understanding fosters empathy, builds trust, and strengthens connections.

✓ **Spark creativity and innovation:** By prompting thoughtful reflection and pushing beyond the expected, open-ended questions can ignite new ideas and spark creative thinking. This dynamic exchange can lead to unexpected discoveries, innovative solutions, and collaborative problem-solving.

✓ **Express genuine interest:** Asking open-ended questions shows that you are genuinely interested in the other person's thoughts and feelings. This simple gesture can make a significant difference in the quality of the conversation and the overall relationship.

Mastering the art:

Asking powerful open-ended questions is an art that can be cultivated with practice. Here are some key tips to remember:

✓ **Choose your words wisely:** Start your questions with phrases like "how," "why," "what," "tell me more," "could you elaborate," or "what is your perspective on this?" These words automatically set the stage for an in-depth response.

✓ **Go beyond the obvious:** Avoid questions that have predictable answers. Instead, probe for deeper insights and encourage the other person to share their unique views.

✓ **Become a master:** Once you receive a response, don't let the conversation stagnate. Ask follow-up questions to clarify, dig deeper, and show continued interest. This demonstrates active listening and encourages further elaboration.

✓ **Embrace the power of silence:** Don't be afraid of silence. Pauses can be powerful tools in conversation, allowing the other person time to process their thoughts and formulate their response.

✓ **Be genuinely curious:** The most powerful open-ended questions stem from genuine interest in the other person and their experiences. When you are truly curious, your questions will naturally be more engaging and thoughtful.

Examples to inspire you:

- ✓ **Instead of:** "Did you enjoy the movie?"
- • **Try:** "What did you think about the movie's message?" or "What was your favorite scene and why?"

- ✓ **Instead of:** "Are you nervous about your presentation?"
- • **Try:** "How do you feel about presenting to the team?" or "What are your biggest concerns about the presentation?"

- ✓ **Instead of:** "What do you do for fun?"
- • **Try:** "Tell me about your favorite hobbies and what you enjoy most about them."

- ✓ **Instead of:** "Do you think this new policy will be effective?"
- • **Try:** "What are your thoughts on the potential impact of this new policy?" or "What are some of the potential challenges and opportunities associated with this policy?"

<u>Conclusion</u>

The benefits of embracing open-ended questions are vast and far-reaching. By incorporating these powerful tools into your conversational repertoire, you can unlock a world of possibilities. You will discover the joy of genuine connection, forge deeper relationships, and gain a richer understanding of the world and the people around you. So, embark on this journey of exploration, embrace the power of open-ended questions, and watch as your conversations transform into enriching and meaningful experiences.

19

CHAPTER 4: The Art of Asking Questions

In the intricate dance of conversation, questions serve as the nimble steps that guide the flow and reveal the depths of connection. More than just gathering information, asking the right questions at the right time can unlock a treasure trove of insights, forge strong bonds, and transform a casual exchange into a truly enriching experience.

Why Questions are the Keys to Conversation

1) **They unlock hidden perspectives**: Imagine a conversation as a vast landscape shrouded in mist. By asking insightful questions, you pierce the veil, revealing the other person's unique worldview, experiences, and beliefs. This allows you to bridge cultural gaps, challenge your own assumptions, and gain a broader understanding of the human tapestry.

2) **They show genuine interest**: A well-placed question is like a soft spotlight that illuminates the other person's individuality. It demonstrates your genuine interest in their thoughts and feelings, fostering a sense of connection and encouraging them to share more openly and honestly.

3) **They encourage deeper thinking**: Unlike closed-ended questions that elicit simple yes or no answers, open-ended inquiries invite the other person to engage in a mental exploration. They prompt them to elaborate, explain their reasoning, and delve deeper into the fabric of the conversation, leading to richer insights and a more meaningful exchange.

20

4) **They keep the conversation flowing:** Imagine a riverbed devoid of water, stagnant and lifeless. Conversation stands to suffer the same fate without the invigorating flow of questions. By skillfully weaving inquiries into the dialogue, you prevent the conversation from becoming one-sided or falling into awkward silences. Instead, you keep the focus on the other person, encouraging their active participation and ensuring the conversation continues to meander forward with a sense of purpose and vibrancy.

Mastering the Art of Asking Questions

1) **Embrace the spirit of inquiry:** Approach each conversation with a genuine thirst for knowledge and understanding. Cultivate a sense of curiosity about the other person's perspective, their experiences, and their unique way of seeing the world.

2) **Listen with an open heart:** Before formulating your question, pause and truly listen to the other person's words and non-verbal cues. This allows you to tailor your question to the specific context of the conversation, ensuring its relevance and impact.

3) **Reach for open-ended questions:** These questions are like the keys that unlock the door to deeper understanding. Instead of "Did you enjoy the movie?" try "What resonated with you most about the film?" or "What thoughts or emotions did it evoke?"

4) **Follow-up is key:** Don't let the conversation end with a single response. Use follow-up questions to explore different angles, clarify points, and encourage further elaboration. This demonstrates your genuine interest and allows the other person to expand on their thoughts and feelings.

5) **Silence is golden:** Sometimes, the most powerful question is no question at all. Learn to leverage the power of silence, allowing the other person space to reflect, gather their thoughts, and formulate their response.

6) **Let your questions reflect your tone:** Ensure your questions are delivered with a genuine, respectful, and inviting tone. Avoid using a condescending or judgmental approach, as this can create an uncomfortable atmosphere and hinder open communication.

7) **Challenge your own assumptions:** Don't shy away from asking questions that may challenge your own beliefs or perspectives. This intellectual

21

exploration can lead to personal growth and a deeper understanding of yourself and the world around you.

8) **Share your own stories:** By weaving your own experiences and stories into the conversation, you create a bridge for connection and encourage the other person to do the same. This fosters a more personal and engaging dialogue.

9) **Practice makes perfect:** The more you practice asking thoughtful questions, the more natural and skilled you will become. Seek opportunities to engage in conversation with diverse individuals in various settings. This allows you to experiment with different question styles and refine your technique.

Conclusion

By internalizing these principles and incorporating them into your conversational repertoire, you can transform yourself from a passive listener to a master conversationalist. You will unlock the full potential of dialogue, forge meaningful connections, and create memories that resonate long after the conversation ends. Remember, the art of asking questions is an ongoing journey of exploration, discovery, and connection. Embrace the learning curve, and watch as your conversations blossom into vibrant expressions of human understanding and shared experience.

CHAPTER 5: Active Listening and Empathy

Imagine two people sitting across from each other at a cafe. One person is talking animatedly, gesturing wildly with their hands. The other sits passively, occasionally nodding their head, but their gaze is fixed on their phone. While words are being exchanged, there's no real connection happening. This is the antithesis of a deep and meaningful conversation.

Active listening and empathy are the vital ingredients missing in this scene. They are the bedrock upon which genuine connection and understanding are built. They are the tools that allow us to transcend the superficial and tap into the richness of another person's experience.

Active listening isn't simply letting the sounds of someone's voice wash over you. It's an active engagement, a conscious effort to be fully present in the moment and absorb the speaker's message in its entirety. It's a symphony of different elements, each playing a crucial role:

- ✓ **Full Attention:** This means silencing the inner critic, putting away distractions like phones, and focusing all your energy on the speaker. Imagine you have a spotlight that illuminates only the person speaking, highlighting their words, emotions, and body language.

- ✓ **Non-Verbal Communication:** Our bodies speak volumes even when our mouths remain silent. Leaning in, maintaining eye contact, and using open postures convey interest and encourage the speaker to share more. Crossing your arms, looking away, or fidgeting can send the opposite message, creating a barrier to connection.

23

- ✓ **Verbal Cues:** Paraphrasing and reflecting back what you've heard is a powerful tool. It ensures understanding, clarifies any confusion, and shows the speaker that you've been paying attention. Imagine holding up a mirror to the speaker's words, reflecting them back with clarity and care.

- ✓ **Open-Ended Questions:** Instead of firing off yes-or-no questions that can be easily shut down, ask questions that invite elaboration and deeper exploration. Think of these as pathways into the speaker's world, opening doors to their thoughts, feelings, and experiences.

Empathy takes active listening a step further. It's about stepping into the speaker's shoes, seeing the world through their eyes, and feeling the emotions that resonate within their words. It's not about agreeing with everything they say, but about understanding their perspective and validating their experience.

Imagine yourself standing on a mountaintop, gazing at the vast landscape below. You see the paths the speaker has walked, the challenges they've faced, and the joys they've experienced. This vantage point allows you to empathize with their journey, even if you haven't walked the same paths yourself.

Empathy manifests in various ways:

- ✓ **Acknowledgment:** Simply acknowledging the speaker's emotions can be incredibly powerful. Saying, "It sounds like you're feeling frustrated" or "I understand why you might be upset" shows that you're paying attention and that their feelings matter.

- ✓ **Validation:** This is about confirming the speaker's experience as legitimate and understandable. It's not about condoning their actions or justifying their feelings, but about creating a safe space for them to express themselves freely.

- ✓ **Emotional Support:** Sometimes, all someone needs is a listening ear and a shoulder to lean on. Offering your support without judgment can provide comfort and help them navigate difficult emotions.

Active listening and empathy are not innate talents; they are skills that can be cultivated and honed with practice. Here are some exercises to help you develop these invaluable skills:

24

- ✓ **Practice mindful listening:** Start by focusing on everyday sounds like the wind rustling through leaves or the birds chirping. This will train your mind to be present and aware of the subtle nuances around you.

- ✓ **Role-playing with a friend:** Assign different scenarios and take turns practicing active listening and empathy. This will allow you to receive feedback and refine your skills in a safe and supportive environment.

- ✓ **Journaling:** Reflect on your interactions with others. Identify moments where you could have practiced active listening or shown more empathy. This will help you become more conscious of your communication patterns.

- ✓ **Seek inspiration from mentors:** Observe individuals who are skilled communicators and pay attention to how they actively listen and empathize with others.

By diligently practicing these skills, you'll find yourself engaging in conversations that go beyond the superficial. You'll build deeper connections, cultivate stronger relationships, and unlock a world of understanding and shared experiences. Remember, the doors to meaningful conversations are opened by the keys of active listening and empathy. So, step into the world of genuine connection and start unlocking the depths of human understanding.

The Art of Asking Questions: Unlocking the Secrets of Engaging Conversations

As important as active listening and empathy are, they are just two pieces of the puzzle. The art of asking questions is the missing piece, the key that unlocks the treasure chest of deep and engaging conversations.

Unlike the closed-ended questions that demand a simple yes or no response, open-ended questions are the lifeblood of meaningful conversations. They act as invitations, beckoning the speaker to open up, share their thoughts and feelings, and embark on a journey of self-discovery.

Imagine yourself holding a magnifying glass, focusing it on a particular aspect of the speaker's story. Open-ended questions allow you to zoom in on their experiences, revealing fascinating details and uncovering hidden emotions.

25

Here are some examples of open-ended questions that can spark insightful conversations:

- ✓ "Tell me more about..." This simple prompt encourages the speaker to elaborate on a specific point, adding depth and richness to their narrative.

- ✓ "How did you feel when...?" This question invites the speaker to tap into their emotions and share their inner world, creating a sense of vulnerability and trust.

- ✓ "What were you thinking when you..." This delves into the speaker's thought process, providing valuable insights into their motivations and perspectives.

- ✓ "Can you explain what you mean by...?" This clarifies any ambiguity and ensures you both are on the same page, fostering deeper understanding.

- ✓ "What questions do you have for me?" This turns the tables, inviting the speaker to actively participate in the conversation and share their own interests and curiosities.

Asking the right questions is an art form, requiring attentiveness and a genuine interest in the speaker. It's about being present in the moment, listening intently, and picking up on subtle cues that reveal potential avenues for exploration.

Here are some additional tips for asking compelling questions:

- ✓ **Be curious, not interrogative.** The goal is to learn and understand, not to test or judge the speaker.

- ✓ **Follow up with additional questions.** Demonstrating your interest by asking clarifying questions shows the speaker you're engaged and invested in their story.

- ✓ **Listen without interrupting.** Give the speaker the space they need to articulate their thoughts and feelings fully.

- ✓ **Ask open-ended questions, but don't be afraid to ask closed-ended questions for clarification or confirmation.**

26

✓ **Be mindful of your tone and body language.** Convey warmth, openness, and genuine interest through your nonverbal cues.

By mastering the art of asking questions, you transform yourself from a passive listener to an active participant in the conversation. You become a guide, leading your companion on a journey of self-discovery and shared understanding. With each question you ask, you unlock a new facet of their experience, enriching your own understanding of the world and forging bonds that transcend the superficial.

So, embrace the power of curiosity. Ask questions that spark meaningful conversations, and unlock the secrets that lie within each individual you encounter. Remember, the most engaging conversations are not one-sided monologues, but dynamic journeys of exploration, co-created through curiosity, empathy, and the art of asking the right questions.

27

CHAPTER 6: The Importance of Non-Verbal Communication

While the words we speak form the foundation of conversation, it's the unspoken language that truly paints the full picture. Our non-verbal communication, encompassing everything from subtle shifts in our posture to the inflection of our voice, plays a critical role in conveying our true thoughts, emotions, and intentions. Mastering this silent language is essential for becoming a truly effective communicator.

Delving Deeper into the Silent Language:

Non-verbal cues can be broadly categorized into four key elements:

1) **Body Language:** Our posture, gestures, and movements are a constant stream of information, often revealing what words might not. Relaxed shoulders and an open posture project confidence and receptivity, while crossed arms and clenched fists can suggest defensiveness or anxiety. Leaning in shows interest and engagement, while fidgeting or looking away can indicate boredom or nervousness. Even the way we cross our legs can offer insights into our personality and comfort level.

2) **Facial Expressions:** Often referred to as the "windows to the soul," our faces are a dynamic map of our emotions. A genuine smile speaks volumes about warmth and happiness, while a furrowed brow might hint at concern or frustration. A raised eyebrow can convey disbelief or surprise, while pursed lips might suggest disapproval or thoughtfulness. Recognizing these subtle changes in facial expressions allows us to understand the emotional undercurrent beneath the spoken word.

28

3) **Paralanguage:** The non-verbal aspects of our speech, including volume, tone, pace, and vocal variety, add depth and nuance to our communication. A monotone voice can make us appear dull and disinterested, while an overly enthusiastic tone might be perceived as insincere or manipulative. Varying our vocal inflection enhances our storytelling, emphasizes key points, and keeps listeners engaged. The speed of our speech can also convey urgency or nervousness, while pauses can be used for dramatic effect or to emphasize important information.

4) **Haptics:** Touch can be a powerful tool for forging connections and conveying emotions that words simply cannot express. A friendly pat on the back can offer encouragement and support, while a comforting hug can provide solace and understanding. A warm handshake can solidify a deal or mark the beginning of a new friendship. However, it's crucial to be mindful of cultural norms and individual preferences to avoid misinterpretations and maintain appropriate boundaries.

Unlocking the Power of Non-Verbal Communication:

Developing strong non-verbal communication skills offers a multitude of advantages in various aspects of our lives:

- ✓ **Enhanced Clarity:** When our words and nonverbal cues are aligned, our message becomes clearer and more impactful. This reduces ambiguity and ensures our message is received as intended.

- ✓ **Building Rapport:** Maintaining eye contact, mirroring body language, and displaying genuine smiles are powerful ways to build trust and connection with others. This fosters a positive environment where communication flows more naturally.

- ✓ **Unveiling True Emotions:** While words can be easily manipulated, nonverbal cues can often reveal our true feelings more authentically. Recognizing these subtle signals helps us understand the genuine emotions behind someone's words and respond accordingly.

- ✓ **Active Listening Skills:** Non-verbal cues such as nodding, leaning in, and maintaining eye contact demonstrate our active listening and encourage the

29

speaker to share more freely. This fosters deeper understanding and creates a more meaningful conversation.

Refining the Art of Non-Verbal Communication:

Mastering the art of non-verbal communication requires conscious effort and dedication. Here are some practical steps you can take:

- ✓ **Become an Observer:** Pay close attention to how others utilize nonverbal communication in different situations. Observe their body language, facial expressions, and tone of voice to gain valuable insights.

- ✓ **The Power of Self-Reflection:** Record yourself having conversations and analyze your own nonverbal cues. This can help you identify areas for improvement and track your progress over time.

- ✓ **Practice Makes Perfect:** Practice your skills in various settings, from casual conversations with friends to formal presentations at work. This will boost your confidence and help you apply your skills effectively in real-world situations.

- ✓ **Feedback is Key:** Seek constructive feedback from trusted friends, colleagues, or even a communication coach. Their honest observations can provide valuable insights and help you refine your non-verbal communication skills.

Unveiling the Untold Story:

Beyond the words we speak, there lies a vast and complex world of non-verbal communication. By actively honing your skills and becoming attuned to the silent language, you can unlock a deeper level of understanding and connection in your interactions with others. You will be able to communicate more effectively, build stronger relationships, and navigate the complexities of human interaction with greater confidence and grace.

Examples:

- ✓ Imagine a first date where two people are genuinely interested in each other. Their bodies naturally lean in towards each other during conversation, their smiles are genuine and frequent, and they maintain warm eye contact. These nonverbal cues silently communicate their attraction and create a sense of intimacy and connection.

- ✓ Imagine a tense negotiation between two business executives. One executive maintains a confident posture, with a firm handshake and direct eye contact. Their voice remains calm and steady, even when faced with challenges. The other executive fidgets and avoids eye contact, their voice betraying their nervousness. Through these contrasting nonverbal cues, the power dynamic of the negotiation becomes evident.

- ✓ Picture a teacher delivering a lecture to a large audience. They use animated gestures and facial expressions to emphasize key points, their voice rising and falling to maintain engagement. They move around the room, making eye contact with different students to ensure everyone feels included. These nonverbal cues create a dynamic learning environment and increase the students' comprehension and retention of information.

- ✓ Consider a young child struggling to express their emotions verbally. Their body language speaks volumes — tears welling up in their eyes, clenched fists, and a trembling chin. A parent, recognizing these nonverbal cues, offers comfort and support, allowing the child to express themselves freely and feel understood.

These examples illustrate the profound impact of non-verbal communication in various situations. By mastering this silent language, we can enhance our interactions with others, build stronger relationships, and navigate the complexities of human interaction with greater ease and effectiveness.

Conclusion

Ultimately, mastering the art of conversation requires a harmonious blend of both verbal and non-verbal communication. When we use words consciously and deliberately, while remaining mindful of the silent language we speak through our body, voice, and demeanor, we unlock the true potential of meaningful and impactful communication.

Remember: non-verbal communication is a dynamic and multifaceted art form. Continuous learning, self-awareness, and a genuine interest in understanding others are key to mastering this powerful tool and becoming a truly exceptional communicator.

31

CHAPTER 7: Overcoming Shyness and Social Anxiety

The prospect of engaging in conversation can send shivers down the spines of even the most articulate individuals. Shyness and social anxiety, like menacing shadows, hold us back from forging meaningful connections and experiencing the joy of genuine conversation. This chapter delves into the depths of these anxieties, offering practical tools and strategies to conquer them and unleash your potential as a confident and engaging conversationalist.

Unpacking the Roots:

Before we embark on our journey of overcoming shyness and social anxiety, we must first understand their origins. These emotions often stem from a deep-seated fear of negative evaluation or judgment. We worry about saying something foolish, appearing awkward, or being misunderstood. This fear can manifest in various ways, from blushing and sweating to shaky hands and racing hearts, further fueling our anxieties and creating a vicious cycle.

Challenging the Inner Critic:

One crucial step in overcoming these anxieties is silencing the harsh inner critic that echoes negativity within our minds. We must replace these self-deprecating thoughts with affirmations that foster self-compassion and confidence. Instead of telling ourselves "I'm boring and no one wants to talk to me," we can counter with "I have valuable things to share and I am worthy of connection." This shift in perspective lays the foundation for developing self-belief and approaching conversations with a more positive outlook.

32

Taking the Plunge with Gradual Exposure:

Like divers conquering the depths, overcoming shyness requires gradual exposure to the very situations that induce anxiety. Start small and take baby steps. Initiating low-pressure conversations with the cashier at your local store, striking up a brief chat with a neighbor about the weather, or joining a conversation in a coffee shop can be excellent starting points. As you gain confidence and experience the ease of these interactions, gradually increase the complexity and duration of your conversations.

Shifting the Focus:

One potent strategy is to shift your focus from your internal anxieties to the person you're interacting with. Ask open-ended questions that spark their interests and listen attentively to their stories and experiences. By actively engaging with them, you take the pressure off yourself and allow the conversation to flow organically. This outward focus also fosters genuine connection and creates a more positive experience for both parties.

Sharpening Your Communication Arsenal:

Just like a skilled craftsman relies on well-honed tools, developing essential communication skills is essential for overcoming shyness and becoming a confident conversationalist. Actively listening to others, conveying your thoughts and feelings effectively through non-verbal communication, and weaving captivating narratives through storytelling are all valuable tools in your communication arsenal. These skills can be honed through joining conversation groups, practicing public speaking, or seeking guidance from online resources.

Embracing the Beautiful Imperfections:

Remember, perfection is a myth perpetuated by unrealistic societal expectations. Everyone makes mistakes, experiences awkward moments, and stumbles through conversations at times. Don't let the fear of imperfection paralyze you. Embrace your unique voice and perspective, even if they don't conform to everyone else's. Authenticity is far more attractive than a fabricated image of flawlessness.

Celebrating Milestones:

Recognizing and celebrating your progress, no matter how small, is crucial for maintaining motivation and self-belief. Did you overcome your initial hesitation and

33

strike up a conversation with a stranger? Did you manage to hold your own in a group discussion? Acknowledge these achievements, big or small, and reward yourself for your efforts. This positive reinforcement will fuel your confidence and drive you forward on your journey.

Seeking Professional Support:

If shyness and social anxiety significantly impact your daily life and hinder you from forming meaningful connections, seeking professional support can be invaluable. Therapists offer a safe and confidential space to explore the root causes of your anxieties and develop personalized strategies for managing them. They can also provide guidance on practicing social skills and building your confidence in social situations.

Additional Tools for Your Toolbox:

Taming the Anxiety Beast: Relaxation techniques such as deep breathing, meditation, and progressive muscle relaxation can help manage anxiety before and during social interactions.

- ✓ **Visualizing Success:** Imagine yourself engaging in confident and enjoyable conversations. This mental rehearsal can prime your mind for positive outcomes and boost your confidence.

- ✓ **Building Your Support Network:** Joining social clubs or groups that align with your interests provides opportunities to practice your communication skills and build a supportive network of individuals.

- ✓ **Rewarding Yourself:** Celebrate your successes, however small, with rewards that reinforce the positive aspects of social interaction. This helps create positive associations with social situations and motivates you to continue making progress.

Overcoming shyness and social anxiety is a journey, not a destination. It requires patience, dedication, and self-compassion. By understanding your anxieties, challenging negative thoughts, and equipping yourself with the tools and strategies outlined in this chapter, you can gradually overcome these obstacles and unlock your potential as a confident and engaging conversationalist. Remember, you are worthy of connection and meaningful conversations. With every hurdle you overcome, you pave the way for a richer and more fulfilling social life.

34

Examples of Conversation Starters:

- ✓ **Open-ended questions:** These questions spark genuine conversation and encourage the other person to share their thoughts and experiences. Examples include: "What have you been passionate about lately?" or "What's the most interesting thing you've learned recently?"

- ✓ **Observational comments:** Making an observation about your surroundings or the other person's attire or accessories can be a natural way to break the ice. For instance, you could say, "I love your necklace! Where did you get it?" or "This coffee shop has such a cozy atmosphere, don't you think?"

- ✓ **Shared experiences:** If you find yourself in a similar situation as someone else, use that as a springboard for conversation. For example, if you're both waiting in line for coffee, you could say, "I can never decide what to get here. What's your favorite drink?"

Beyond Words: The Power of Non-Verbal Communication:

Non-verbal communication plays a crucial role in fostering connection and conveying your message effectively. Maintain good eye contact, smile genuinely, and use open body language like uncrossed arms and an upright posture. These subtle cues communicate confidence and interest, creating a more inviting and engaging presence.

The Art of Storytelling:

Humans are wired for stories. Sharing personal narratives allows us to connect with others on a deeper level and build rapport. When crafting your story, focus on details that evoke emotion and paint a vivid picture for your listener. Remember, authenticity and vulnerability are key to captivating storytelling.

Navigating Difficult Topics:

Not all conversations are sunshine and roses. At times, you may find yourself navigating challenging topics that evoke strong emotions. In such situations, it's crucial to approach the conversation with empathy and respect for the other person's perspective. Actively listen to their point of view, acknowledge their feelings, and express your own thoughts and opinions in a calm and respectful manner.

Turning Awkward Silences into Opportunities:

Awkward silences are a natural part of any conversation. Instead of letting them fill you with anxiety, learn to embrace them as opportunities to reflect and re-engage. Take a deep breath, smile, and use the silence as a springboard to ask a follow-up question or share a related thought.

Conflict Resolution: Turning Differences into Dialogue:

Disagreements are inevitable in any relationship. When faced with conflict, remember to stay calm and communicate assertively. Focus on the issue at hand, avoid personal attacks, and actively listen to the other person's perspective. Seek common ground and work together to find a solution that works for both of you.

The Art of Ending Conversations:

Saying goodbye gracefully is just as important as initiating a conversation. Avoid abrupt endings and instead, look for natural points to conclude the interaction. Thank the person for their time and conversation, and express your desire to connect again soon. A genuine farewell leaves a lasting positive impression.

The Power of Conversation: Building Bridges and Connecting Hearts

The ability to engage in meaningful conversation is a superpower, enriching our lives in countless ways. It allows us to build strong relationships, exchange ideas, learn from others, and experience the joy of human connection.

Final Thoughts:

Overcoming shyness and social anxiety takes courage, but the rewards are immeasurable. By embracing the strategies outlined in this chapter and embarking on a journey of self-discovery and personal growth, you can unlock your potential as a confident and engaging conversationalist. Remember, you are not alone on this journey. There are resources available to support you every step of the way, and with dedication and perseverance, you can achieve your goals and build a life filled with meaningful connections and enriching conversations.

Start engaging today, one conversation at a time, and witness the transformation within yourself and the world around you.

Conclusion

36

Overcoming shyness and social anxiety is not a linear path. There will be moments of triumph and moments of doubt. There will be days you feel like a social butterfly, flitting from conversation to conversation with ease, and days you feel like a caterpillar, curled up in a cocoon of self-consciousness. But through it all, remember this: progress, not perfection, is the goal.

Embrace the journey. Celebrate the small victories, like holding eye contact for a few seconds longer than usual or initiating a conversation with someone new. Learn from your setbacks, analyze what triggered your anxieties, and use those experiences as stepping stones towards greater confidence.

Remember, you are not defined by your anxieties. You are a unique individual with valuable thoughts, opinions, and experiences to share. Allow yourself to shine through your conversations, and don't be afraid to let your authentic self be heard.

As you embark on this journey, you will discover a hidden world of connections, laughter, and learning. You will find yourself forging meaningful friendships, building bridges with diverse individuals, and expanding your horizons in ways you never imagined. Conversation is not just a way to pass time; it is a powerful tool for building a richer, more fulfilling life.

So, open your heart, open your mind, and open yourself to the possibilities that await. Take the first step, initiate the first conversation, and watch as the world unfolds before you in its vibrant, interconnected beauty. Remember, the most captivating conversations often begin with a single question, a simple smile, or the courage to step outside your comfort zone.

Now, go forth and embrace the art of conversation. The world is waiting to hear your story.

CHAPTER 8: Building Rapport and Trust

Building rapport and trust is not just a fancy phrase – it's the very foundation of any meaningful conversation. Imagine a garden: without fertile soil and nurturing conditions, no beautiful flower can blossom. Similarly, without rapport and trust, communication remains shallow, guarded, and unfulfilling. It's the essential ingredient that allows true connection and deeper understanding to bloom.

Why is Building Rapport and Trust So Important?

Think about the most enriching conversations you've had. What made them so special? Chances are, you felt a sense of safety and comfort, allowing you to express yourself freely and authentically. This feeling of security and connection stems directly from rapport and trust.

Here's why building rapport and trust is crucial:

1) **Creates a Safe Space for Openness and Honesty:** When you feel safe and comfortable with someone, you're more likely to share your true thoughts and feelings. This vulnerability and intimacy are vital for building deeper, more meaningful connections.

2) **Sparks Curiosity and Learning:** When we trust someone, we're more receptive to their perspectives and ideas, even if they differ from our own. This openness fosters intellectual curiosity and personal growth as we expand our understanding of the world and ourselves.

3) **Strengthens Relationships and Builds Networks:** Strong relationships are the bedrock of a fulfilling life, and they all share a common foundation: trust and rapport. These bonds offer support, encouragement, and a sense of belonging, enriching our lives in countless ways.

Building Rapport and Trust: Your Practical Toolkit

Now that we understand the importance of rapport and trust, let's delve into the practical steps you can take to cultivate them:

1) **Be Yourself, Unapologetically:** People can easily detect insincerity. When you embrace your authentic self in your interactions, you project a trustworthy and approachable persona that invites connection.

2) **Show Genuine Interest:** This isn't just about asking questions; it's about actively listening, focusing on their responses, and demonstrating that you value their thoughts and experiences.

3) **Cultivate Empathy:** Stepping into another person's shoes and acknowledging their feelings fosters a sense of shared experience and connection, building trust and understanding.

4) **Respect and Non-Judgement Go Hand-in-Hand:** Everyone has unique experiences and perspectives. Create a safe space where everyone feels comfortable expressing themselves without fear of criticism.

5) **Consistency is Key:** Trust is built over time through consistent behavior. Follow through on your commitments and keep promises – this demonstrates your reliability and trustworthiness.

6) **Find Common Ground:** Shared interests or experiences are powerful connectors. Look for those commonalities and use them to build rapport and ease the flow of conversation.

7) **Speak with Your Body:** Positive body language like eye contact, smiles, and leaning in shows engagement and interest, creating a welcoming environment for deeper connection.

8) **Non-Verbal Cues Matter:** Remember, 93% of communication happens nonverbally. Be mindful of your body language, facial expressions, and tone of voice, ensuring they align with your message.

39

9) **Patience is a Virtue**: Building rapport and trust takes time and effort. Don't expect instant results. Be patient, consistent, and genuine, and trust will naturally blossom.

Beyond the Basics: Advanced Techniques

Building rapport and trust is an ongoing journey, and there's always more to learn:

1) **Open-Ended Questions Unlock Deeper Conversations**: Replace closed-ended questions with open-ended ones that invite elaboration and encourage deeper dialogue.

2) **Personal Stories Bridge the Gap**: Sharing personal anecdotes and experiences reveals vulnerability and builds trust. This creates a sense of connection and allows others to see the real you.

3) **Offer Positive Reinforcement**: Acknowledge their contributions, offer compliments, and show appreciation. This positive reinforcement strengthens connections and fosters a more enjoyable interaction.

4) **Listen Actively, Avoid Dominating**: Give others their space and time to express themselves without interrupting. This shows respect and encourages further interaction.

5) **Cultural Sensitivity is Key**: Be aware of cultural differences and adapt your communication style accordingly. This demonstrates respect and appreciation for their unique background.

Remember, Building Rapport and Trust is a Two-Way Street

While it's essential to employ these strategies, it's crucial to remember that building rapport and trust is a reciprocal process. Create a safe space where others feel comfortable reciprocating your efforts, fostering genuine connections and enriching conversations.

Examples: Putting Theory into Practice

✓ **Scenario 1: Networking Event Jitters**

40

You're at a networking event, surrounded by unfamiliar faces, feeling nervous and unsure how to initiate conversations.

Action: Take a deep breath, approach someone, introduce yourself with a warm smile, and ask a question about their work or interests. Actively listen to their response and ask follow-up questions. This genuine interest and initiative will break the ice and create a foundation for further connection.

Outcome: By showing interest and creating a safe space for conversation, you build rapport and trust, making the interaction more enjoyable and potentially leading to new professional opportunities.

✓ **Scenario 2: Navigating Difficult Conversations**

You're having a difficult conversation with a loved one, discussing a sensitive topic that leads to disagreement.

Action: Actively listen without interrupting or judging. Try to see things from their perspective and offer empathy. Acknowledge their feelings and validate their experience. Focus on finding common ground and understanding their point of view.

Outcome: By approaching the conversation with respect and understanding, you build trust and create a space for open and honest communication. This can lead to a resolution, strengthen your relationship, and deepen your connection.

Building Rapport and Trust: A Lifelong Journey

Building rapport and trust is not a destination; it's a continuous journey. It requires ongoing effort, commitment, and a willingness to learn and adapt. By incorporating these strategies into your daily interactions, you can cultivate meaningful connections, enrich your life, and build lasting relationships that bring joy and fulfillment.

Remember, communication is an art, and like any art form, it takes practice and dedication to master. As you embark on this journey of building rapport and trust, embrace the process, learn from each interaction, and allow yourself to connect with others on a deeper level. The rewards will be immeasurable.

Building Rapport and Trust in Different Contexts

While the core principles of building rapport and trust remain consistent across different situations, the specific techniques you employ will vary depending on the context. Here are some examples:

1) **Networking Events:**

   ✓ **Start small talks:** In large gatherings, initiate brief conversations with several individuals. Ask simple questions about their work, hobbies, or the event itself. This helps ease into interactions and build initial rapport.

   ✓ **Use the environment to your advantage:** Leverage the event theme, refreshments, or decorations as conversation starters. Shared experiences create common ground and facilitate deeper interaction.

   ✓ **Be mindful of time:** Respect others' time and keep conversations concise. Remember, the goal is to make a positive impression and build initial rapport, not delve into lengthy discussions.

2) **Job Interviews:**

   ✓ **Express genuine interest in the company and position.** Ask thoughtful questions about the role, the team, and the company culture. This demonstrates your enthusiasm and initiative.

   ✓ **Highlight relevant skills and experiences.** Share specific examples of past successes that showcase your capabilities and align with the job requirements.

   ✓ **Show your enthusiasm and passion.** Exude energy and excitement about the opportunity. This conveys your genuine interest and commitment to the role.

3) **Romantic Relationships:**

   ✓ **Be open and vulnerable.** Share your thoughts, feelings, and experiences authentically. This fosters trust and intimacy.

42

✓ **Actively listen and offer support.** Be empathetic and understanding, providing a safe space for your partner to express themselves freely.

✓ **Plan meaningful date nights.** Go beyond routine activities and create shared experiences that strengthen your bond and foster deeper connection.

4) **Difficult Conversations:**

✓ **Acknowledge the discomfort.** Acknowledge the tension and express your desire for a constructive conversation. This helps set expectations and create a safe space for dialogue.

✓ **Focus on "I" statements.** Instead of assigning blame, express your own feelings and experiences. This reduces defensiveness and encourages open communication.

✓ **Focus on finding solutions together.** Approach the conversation as a team, working collaboratively to find mutually agreeable solutions.

5) **Cross-Cultural Interactions:**

✓ **Be mindful of cultural differences.** Research and respect cultural norms, communication styles, and nonverbal cues to avoid misunderstandings.

✓ **Show genuine interest in their culture.** Ask questions about their traditions, values, and customs. This demonstrates respect and appreciation for their unique background.

✓ **Be patient and understanding.** Cultural differences can lead to miscommunications. Allow yourself and the other person time to adjust and understand each other's perspectives.

Remember, Building Rapport and Trust is a Continual Process

Building rapport and trust is a dynamic process that evolves over time. As you engage in different interactions and meet new people, you will encounter diverse

43

situations and personalities. Be adaptable, learn from each experience, and refine your communication skills to build stronger and more meaningful connections with everyone you encounter.

By embracing the art of building rapport and trust, you open yourself up to a world of possibilities. You'll experience richer conversations, forge deeper relationships, and ultimately lead a more fulfilling life. So, go forth, connect with others, and enjoy the journey!

Conclusion

In the grand tapestry of human interaction, few threads hold as much power as rapport and trust. They are the invisible threads that bind us together, weaving connections that enrich our lives and fuel our growth. Through genuine interest, empathy, and respect, we build bridges that allow us to cross over into the hearts and minds of others.

Building rapport and trust isn't about quick fixes or superficial interactions. It's about cultivating an authentic presence, demonstrating genuine care, and creating a space where vulnerability and honesty can flourish. It's about embracing the messiness of human connection, with all its imperfections and imperfections, and fostering a sense of shared humanity.

The rewards of this journey are immeasurable. Deeper connections lead to stronger relationships, whether with friends, family, colleagues, or even strangers. It fosters a sense of belonging and community, reminding us that we are not alone in this vast world. It opens doors to new opportunities, allows us to learn from diverse perspectives, and ultimately expands our understanding of ourselves and the world around us.

As you embark on this continuous journey, remember to approach it with curiosity, patience, and a genuine desire to connect. Let go of expectations and embrace the spontaneous beauty of authentic interaction. Celebrate the joy of shared laughter and the solace of knowing that you are truly seen and heard.

With each conversation, with each interaction, build upon the foundation of trust and rapport. Weave these threads into the fabric of your life, and watch as your world becomes a tapestry of vibrant connections, meaningful experiences, and lasting joy.

44

Remember, the power to build rapport and trust lies within each of us. Go forth, share your light with the world, and connect with others on a deeper level. The impact you make will ripple outwards, creating a world where connection thrives, and the human spirit truly flourishes.

45

CHAPTER 9: Starting Conversations with Confidence

The first few moments of any interaction hold immense power. They set the tone for the entire conversation and determine whether a genuine connection will blossom or wither away. Initiating these crucial first moments can be daunting for even the most seasoned communicator, but it's a skill that anyone can master. In this chapter, we'll delve into the art of starting conversations with confidence, transforming those initial anxieties into opportunities for meaningful and lasting connections.

Understanding the Fear: A Natural Human Response

The fear of starting conversations is rooted in deep-seated human anxieties. We worry about judgment, rejection, and feeling inadequate. These fears are natural and serve a purpose - they protect us from potential harm. However, it's important to acknowledge these anxieties without letting them paralyze us. Instead of fighting them, we can learn to manage them and focus on the positive aspects of connecting with others.

Shifting Your Mindset: From Fear to Curiosity

Instead of dwelling on the potential negativity, cultivate a mindset of curiosity and openness. View each conversation as an adventure, an opportunity to discover new perspectives and expand your world. Imagine the joy of forging a genuine connection and the enriching insights you might gain from the conversation. By focusing on these positive outcomes, you can shift your fear into excitement and anticipation.

46

Preparing for the Spark: Building Confidence through Knowledge

While spontaneity can spark delightful interactions, a little preparation can go a long way in boosting your confidence. Before stepping into a social environment, take some time to reflect on the people you might meet and potential conversation topics. Consider your own interests and passions; identifying common ground will provide natural conversation starters and ease those initial awkward moments.

First Impressions: The Art of Non-Verbal Communication

Remember, first impressions matter. Before you even utter a word, your body language speaks volumes. Stand tall with good posture, make eye contact with a warm smile, and project an aura of confidence. These subtle gestures radiate openness and approachability, inviting others to engage with you.

Open the Door: Sparking Conversation with Open-Ended Questions

Forget about lengthy introductions and scripted lines. Opt for open-ended questions that encourage the other person to share their thoughts and experiences. This fosters engagement and allows the conversation to flow naturally. Ask questions like, "What brought you here today?" or "What are you most passionate about?" These simple inquiries open doors to meaningful and engaging conversations.

Leveraging Your Surroundings: Finding Conversation Starters in the Environment

Your surroundings offer a treasure trove of conversation starters. Use the event you're attending, the weather, or even the artwork on the wall as springboards for engaging discussions. This allows you to find common ground and establish a connection based on shared experiences.

Being Authentic: The Power of Genuine Expression

People crave authenticity. Avoid using scripted lines or adopting personas that feel inauthentic. Instead, let your true personality shine through and be present in the moment. Share your genuine thoughts and feelings, and allow the conversation to unfold organically.

Embracing Silence: The Power of Pauses

47

Silence can be a powerful tool in conversation. It allows for reflection, deeper understanding, and anticipation. Don't feel pressured to fill every gap with chatter. Embrace silence as a natural pause in the flow of conversation, and allow the dialogue to unfold at its own pace.

Practice Makes Progress: Building Confidence Through Experience

Like any skill, starting conversations with confidence takes practice. Step outside your comfort zone and initiate conversations with people you don't know. Join social events, strike up conversations in line at the coffee shop, or simply say hello to your neighbor. The more you practice, the easier and more natural it will become.

Celebrating Your Victories: Recognizing Your Achievements

Acknowledge and celebrate your successes, no matter how small. Each conversation started with confidence is a victory. This positive reinforcement will build your momentum and fuel your confidence for future interactions. Remember, starting conversations is not about achieving perfection; it's about connecting with others and fostering genuine relationships.

Conclusion

By embracing the tips and strategies outlined in this chapter, you can unlock the power of starting conversations with confidence. Replace anxieties with curiosity, prepare the ground for meaningful interactions, and embark on a journey of enriching and lasting connections.

CHAPTER 10: Keeping the Conversation Flowing

Building rapport and engaging someone in conversation is just the first step. Now, you face the challenge of keeping that momentum going, avoiding the dreaded silences and awkward dead ends. A good conversation is like a well-choreographed dance, where both partners actively participate and respond to each other's cues. Let's explore some techniques to keep your conversations flowing and engaging.

1) **The power of open-ended questions:**

These are your conversation lifelines! Unlike closed-ended questions that require a simple yes or no answer, open-ended ones invite elaboration and encourage the other person to share their thoughts, experiences, and opinions. Think of them as invitations to delve deeper and explore the topic at hand.

Here are some examples of open-ended questions:

- ✓ Instead of: "Did you enjoy the movie?"
- • Try: "What were your thoughts on the ending of the movie?"

- ✓ Instead of: "Do you like this music?"
- • Try: "How did you discover this band?"

- ✓ Instead of: "Have you ever been to Paris?"
- • Try: "Tell me about your favorite travel experiences."

49

2) **Active listening and follow-up comments:**

Active listening goes beyond simply hearing the words. It's about demonstrating genuine interest and engagement through your body language and verbal cues. Maintain eye contact, nod your head, and offer encouraging sounds like "uh-huh" or "interesting." When they pause, don't rush to fill the silence. Instead, process what they said and offer thoughtful follow-up comments that show you were paying attention.

Here are some examples of follow-up comments:

- ✓ "That sounds challenging. What were some of the biggest obstacles you faced?"
- ✓ "I can relate to what you're saying. I had a similar experience once."
- ✓ "That's a fascinating perspective. I hadn't thought of it that way before."

3) **Building on common ground:**

As the conversation progresses, find shared interests, experiences, or opinions. This "common ground" provides a natural springboard to keep the dialogue flowing. Mention a related anecdote, ask a question about their experience, or share your own perspective on the topic.

Here are some examples of building on common ground:

- ✓ "I love that book too! What was your favorite scene?"
- ✓ "I'm also interested in learning more about [shared interest]. Do you have any recommendations?"
- ✓ "That reminds me of a time when I..."

4) **Storytelling goes a long way:**

Humans are hardwired for stories. Sharing a personal anecdote or a relevant story can instantly inject life into the conversation and captivate your listener. Choose stories that are relevant to the topic at hand, engaging, and have a clear point. Think about the narrative arc, the characters, and how your story can add value to the conversation.

Here are some examples of using storytelling:

50

✓ "I was once in a similar situation, and..."
✓ "Did you hear about the time when..."
✓ "This story perfectly illustrates what I mean by..."

5) **Embrace curiosity and ask follow-up questions:**

Don't be afraid to ask questions that arise from your genuine curiosity. This shows your interest and encourages further conversation. Pay attention to details mentioned by the other person and use them to ask insightful questions that delve deeper into the topic.

Here are some examples of using curiosity to ask follow-up questions:

✓ "I'm curious about what motivated you to..."
✓ "Can you tell me more about...?"
✓ "I'm interested in understanding your perspective on..."

6) **Be present and engaged:**

Put away your phone, maintain eye contact, and avoid distractions. Show genuine interest in the conversation and the person you're talking to. Your nonverbal cues play a significant role in keeping the conversation flowing. Smile, nod, and use open body language.

7) **Handle silences gracefully:**

Not every pause needs to be filled with words. Sometimes, a comfortable silence can be a powerful tool for reflection and shared understanding. Don't feel pressured to fill every gap with chatter. Embrace the silence and let the conversation unfold naturally.

8) **Be flexible and adapt:**

Conversations are dynamic and unpredictable. Be flexible and willing to adapt to the flow of the conversation. Don't be afraid to change topics if the conversation naturally shifts direction. Sometimes, tangents can lead to unexpected and interesting discoveries.

9) **Know when to end the conversation:**

51

Just as important as starting a conversation is knowing when to gracefully end it. Pay attention to nonverbal cues, watch for natural pauses, and politely wrap up the conversation on a positive note. You can express your enjoyment of the conversation, mention your need to move on, or suggest connecting again in the future.

10) Use humor strategically:

Humor can be a powerful tool to lighten the mood and create a sense of connection. However, use humor carefully. Consider your audience, the context of the conversation, and avoid offensive jokes or sarcasm. A well-placed joke can break the ice, but inappropriate humor can quickly derail the conversation.

11) Be aware of cultural differences:

Cultural differences can influence communication styles and expectations. Be mindful of these differences and adjust your communication accordingly. For example, in some cultures, silence is considered respectful, while in others, it can be interpreted as disinterest. Pay attention to nonverbal cues and adjust your pace and volume accordingly.

12) Avoid dominating the conversation:

While it's important to contribute to the conversation, remember to give the other person space to share their thoughts and experiences. Avoid talking over them or monopolizing the conversation. Be an active listener and encourage them to talk about themselves.

13) Don't be afraid of silence:

Silences aren't always awkward. They can be valuable opportunities for reflection and processing information. Don't feel pressured to fill every pause with words. Instead, enjoy the silence and let the conversation unfold naturally.

14) Be comfortable with pauses:

There's no need to feel rushed to fill every silence. Pausing allows you to process what the other person has said and formulate your response. It also gives them time to respond and contribute to the conversation.

15) Be genuine and authentic:

People can sense when someone is being fake or inauthentic. Be yourself, be genuine in your interactions, and let your personality shine through. People are more likely to connect with you and engage in a meaningful conversation when they feel you are being real.

16) Be confident:

Confidence is key to keeping conversations flowing. Even if you're feeling nervous, project confidence through your body language and voice. Believe in yourself and your ability to have a good conversation.

17) Be patient:

Developing strong conversational skills takes time and practice. Don't get discouraged if you encounter awkward silences or challenging conversations. Be patient with yourself and focus on learning and improving.

18) Practice regularly:

The more you practice engaging in conversations, the more comfortable and skilled you will become. Seek opportunities to talk to people from different backgrounds and walks of life. This will help you develop your conversational skills and broaden your perspective.

19) Learn from your mistakes:

Everyone makes mistakes in conversations. Don't dwell on them. Instead, learn from them and use them as opportunities to improve your communication skills. Reflect on what went wrong and how you can avoid making the same mistake in the future.

Conclusion

Keeping conversations flowing is a skill that anyone can develop with practice and effort. By incorporating these tips and strategies, you can build meaningful

53

connections with others, engage in enjoyable conversations, and leave a lasting positive impression.

CHAPTER 11: Finding Common Ground

In the intricate dance of conversation, few steps hold greater importance than finding common ground. It is the bridge that connects two individuals, transcending differences and building a foundation for a more meaningful exchange. It allows us to see beyond the surface, to discover the shared threads that bind us, and to find a sense of connection in what might otherwise appear to be a vast and isolating world.

The Profound Impact of Finding Common Ground:

The benefits of finding common ground extend far beyond mere politeness. It is a powerful tool that can significantly impact our lives in numerous ways:

- ✓ **Reduced anxiety and stress:** When we feel connected to someone, the inherent anxieties and stress associated with social interaction diminish. The sense of shared understanding creates a relaxed and comfortable atmosphere, allowing us to be ourselves and engage in genuine conversation without feeling self-conscious.

- ✓ **Enhanced trust and rapport:** Discovering shared interests, values, or experiences fosters a sense of trust and rapport that transcends initial impressions. We begin to see each other as allies, individuals with whom we have something in common, rather than strangers to approach with caution. This opens doors to deeper discussions and builds a stronger foundation for a lasting connection.

- ✓ **Broader understanding and perspective:** Finding common ground allows us to step outside our own bubble and explore different perspectives. We gain a deeper understanding of other people's experiences, appreciate the

55

nuances of their viewpoints, and recognize the shared humanity that connects us all. This broadened perspective fosters empathy, tolerance, and a more inclusive worldview.

- ✓ **Facilitated problem-solving and conflict resolution:** When faced with disagreements or challenges, finding common ground helps us identify areas of agreement and build consensus. This shared understanding lays the groundwork for collaborative problem-solving and facilitates finding solutions that work for everyone involved. It allows us to approach conflict with a sense of understanding and cooperation, leading to more positive outcomes.

- ✓ **Increased happiness and well-being:** The positive emotions associated with connection, belonging, and understanding have a significant impact on our overall well-being. When we find common ground with others, we experience greater happiness, satisfaction, and a sense of purpose in life.

Unlocking the Secrets of Finding Common Ground:

While some people seem to possess an innate ability to connect with anyone, finding common ground is a skill that can be learned and honed with practice. Here are some effective strategies to unlock its potential:

1) **Become an Active Listener:**

   - ✓ Pay close attention to both the verbal and nonverbal cues the other person is giving.

   - ✓ Ask clarifying questions and paraphrase their words to confirm your understanding.

   - ✓ Show genuine interest in their thoughts, experiences, and feelings.

   - ✓ Actively listen not just to their words, but also to the emotions and stories behind them.

2) **Ask Open-Ended Questions:**

   - ✓ Go beyond superficial inquiries that invite "yes" or "no" answers.

56

✓ Delve deeper with open-ended questions that encourage elaboration and reveal deeper insights.

✓ Ask questions that encourage them to share their stories, values, opinions, and aspirations.

✓ This allows you to discover hidden commonalities and create a more engaging conversation.

3) **Look Beyond the Obvious:**

✓ Don't limit your search for common ground to superficial similarities like age, profession, or hobbies.

✓ Explore shared values, aspirations, life experiences, or even personal philosophies.

✓ Often, the most meaningful connections lie beneath the surface, waiting to be discovered.

✓ Ask yourself: What are we both passionate about? What are our hopes and dreams for the future? What challenges have we both faced?

4) **Cultivate Curiosity and Open-Mindedness:**

✓ Approach conversations with a genuine desire to learn and understand the other person's perspective.

✓ Be open to new ideas and different ways of thinking.

✓ Avoid judging or criticizing, and instead, embrace the opportunity to broaden your understanding of the world through their eyes.

✓ Remember, even if you disagree on certain things, there is always something to learn from each other.

5) **Share Your Own Story:**

✓ Don't hesitate to share your own experiences, thoughts, and feelings.

57

✓ By opening up and being vulnerable, you invite the other person to do the same.

✓ This reciprocal sharing can create a powerful sense of connection and reveal unexpected commonalities.

✓ Sharing your story also allows the other person to understand you better and build a deeper connection.

6) **Celebrate the Differences:**

✓ While finding common ground is important, appreciating and embracing differences is equally valuable.

✓ Differences can spark stimulating conversations, broaden perspectives, and lead to personal growth.

✓ Instead of focusing solely on similarities, see differences as opportunities to learn and expand your worldview.

7) **Cultivate Patience and Persistence:**

✓ Don't get discouraged if you don't click with someone immediately. Building rapport and finding common ground takes time and effort.

✓ Be patient, continue to engage in conversation, and allow the connection to develop naturally.

✓ Remember, some of the most meaningful relationships are built over time and require consistent nurturing.

Examples of Finding Common Ground:

1) **Crossing Cultural Barriers:**

✓ Imagine meeting someone from a vastly different cultural background. You might start by exploring your shared love for music or food. Discovering common artists or favorite dishes can break the ice and create a sense of connection.

58

✓ As the conversation progresses, you might delve deeper into cultural traditions and values. Sharing stories about family customs or religious beliefs can foster a deeper understanding of their perspective and your own.

✓ Through open-mindedness and a willingness to learn, even the most diverse individuals can find common ground and build a bridge across cultural divides.

2) **Bridging Generational Gaps:**

✓ Sometimes, the most enriching conversations occur between individuals from different generations. A young person might connect with an older individual through their shared passion for history or literature.

✓ Discussing past events or classic works of art allows them to learn from each other's experiences and perspectives.

✓ Similarly, an older person might find common ground with a younger person through their shared interest in technology or social justice.

✓ By engaging in open dialogue and mutual respect, individuals from different generations can overcome stereotypes and build meaningful relationships that benefit both parties.

3) **Finding Common Ground in Conflict:**

✓ Even in the midst of disagreements or conflict, finding common ground can be crucial to resolving issues and finding common solutions.

✓ Identifying areas of shared concern or mutual goals can provide a starting point for constructive dialogue.

✓ By focusing on shared interests rather than differences, conflicting parties can work together to find solutions that satisfy everyone involved.

59

- ✓ This is the essence of collaborative problem-solving and conflict resolution, where finding common ground is the cornerstone for building a stronger, more resilient community.

4) **Fostering Connection in the Workplace:**

   - ✓ Effective communication and collaboration are essential for a successful workplace.

   - ✓ Finding common ground among colleagues can boost team morale, improve productivity, and lead to more creative solutions.

   - ✓ Participating in team-building activities, sharing personal stories, and celebrating individual strengths and achievements can foster a sense of belonging and camaraderie.

   - ✓ By recognizing and appreciating their shared goals and commitment to the organization's success, colleagues can build strong working relationships and achieve their full potential.

Conclusion

Finding common ground is a powerful tool that can unlock doors to meaningful connections, foster understanding, and enrich our lives in countless ways. By incorporating these strategies into your conversations and approaching every interaction with curiosity and open-mindedness, you can build bridges across differences, cultivate lasting relationships, and create a more connected and compassionate world.

CHAPTER 12: The Art of Storytelling

Among the many tools in the conversationalist's arsenal, few shine brighter than the art of storytelling. Stories hold the power to captivate attention, ignite emotions, forge connections, and transfer information in a way that mere words alone cannot. In this chapter, we delve into the intricate tapestry of storytelling, exploring its transformative role in conversations.

Why Stories Matter:

- ✓ **Captivating Attention:** A well-told story transcends mere words, transporting your listener to another world. It becomes an immersive experience, holding their attention captive and leaving them eager to hear more.

  Example: Imagine yourself sitting around a campfire, listening to an elder recount tales of their youth. The crackling fire, the darkness of the night, and the captivating voice weave a spell, drawing you into their world and leaving you breathless with anticipation for the next twist in the tale.

- ✓ **Evoking Emotions:** Stories are emotional journeys, weaving through laughter, tears, and everything in between. They allow us to connect with the characters, feel their joys and sorrows, and experience a range of emotions that resonate with our own.

  Example: Think of a movie that made you cry or a book that brought you to tears of joy. The characters' trials and triumphs became your own, allowing you to experience the full spectrum of human emotions through their story.

61

✓ **Building Connections:** Sharing stories creates a bridge between individuals, fostering a sense of intimacy and vulnerability. It allows us to peek into each other's lives, understand their experiences and values, and forge deeper connections that transcend mere words.

Example: Imagine sitting down with a friend and sharing a childhood memory. As you recount the details, you laugh and reminisce, creating a shared experience that strengthens your bond and brings you closer together.

✓ **Transmitting Information:** By weaving information into a narrative framework, stories make complex ideas more engaging and easier to recall. They become memorable packages of knowledge, allowing us to learn and retain information in a way that dry facts alone cannot.

Example: Think of historical events learned through captivating biographies or scientific concepts explained through engaging parables. The stories act as vessels, transporting knowledge and making it relatable and accessible.

Elements of a Captivating Story:

✓ **Opening Hook:** A compelling story starts strong, grabbing your listener's attention from the very first sentence. It could be a thought-provoking question, a vivid image, or a dramatic statement that sets the stage for the journey to come.

Example: Imagine a story beginning with, "The old woman held the photograph, her eyes tracing the faded lines of her youthful self. What secrets did it hold?" This opening hook sparks curiosity and sets the stage for a captivating tale.

✓ **Clear Narrative Arc:** A strong story needs a well-defined structure. It should have a clear beginning, middle, and end, with a logical progression of events building suspense and leading to a satisfying resolution.

Example: Think of a classic fairy tale, where the hero embarks on a quest, faces challenges, overcomes obstacles, and ultimately achieves a goal. The clear narrative arc keeps the listener engaged and eager to see how the story unfolds.

✓ **Vivid Details:** Sensory details paint a picture with words, bringing your story to life. By describing sights, sounds, smells, tastes, and textures, you create a multi-dimensional experience that immerses your listener in the narrative.

Example: Imagine a character walking through a forest at dusk. Instead of simply saying it's dark, describe the rustle of leaves underfoot, the fading light filtering through the canopy, and the earthy smell of damp soil. This level of detail allows the listener to experience the scene alongside the character.

✓ **Engaging Characters:** Stories are driven by characters who resonate with the audience. They should be relatable, possessing distinct personalities, motivations, and even flaws that make them feel human and real.

Example: Think of your favorite fictional characters. What qualities make them stand out? Is it their bravery, their humor, their kindness, or their resilience? These well-developed characters are what make us connect with the story on a deeper level.

✓ **Natural Dialogue:** The characters' conversations should flow naturally, reflecting their personalities and adding depth to the story. Avoid stilted dialogue that sounds forced or unrealistic.

Example: Imagine two friends catching up over coffee. Their conversation should be filled with natural pauses, interruptions, and colloquialisms that reflect their real-life interactions. This creates a sense of authenticity and draws the listener into the story.

✓ **Meaningful Message:** Beyond the entertainment, every story should have a point. What message do you want your listener to carry with them? What values do you want to convey through your narrative?

Example: Think of a story that encourages kindness, perseverance, or forgiveness. The underlying message adds depth and purpose to the tale, making it more than just mere entertainment. It becomes a catalyst for reflection and personal growth.

Storytelling Techniques:

63

✓ **Personal Anecdotes:** Sharing stories from your own life adds a layer of authenticity and allows you to connect with your listener on a personal level. They can serve as illustrations of your points, adding credibility and depth to your narrative.

Example: Imagine sharing a story about overcoming a fear or learning a valuable lesson. By drawing from your personal experiences, you create a sense of trust and relatability, making your story more impactful.

✓ **Humor:** A well-timed joke can lighten the mood, build rapport, and make your story more engaging. However, humor should be appropriate for the audience and used sparingly to avoid overshadowing the message of your story.

Example: Think of a story that incorporates a witty anecdote or a humorous observation. Laughter can break the tension, create a sense of connection, and make your narrative more memorable.

✓ **Figurative Language:** Utilizing metaphors, similes, and other figures of speech can add depth and imagery to your storytelling. They allow you to paint vivid pictures with words, creating a more engaging and impactful narrative.

Example: Imagine describing a character's eyes as "pools of molten gold" or a sunset as "a canvas painted with fiery hues." This figurative language adds a layer of artistry to your story, making it more evocative and memorable.

✓ **Varying Pace and Tone:** Monotony is the enemy of engagement. Vary your pace and tone throughout your story to keep your listener captivated. Emphasize key points, slow down for dramatic moments, and speak with passion to convey the emotions of your narrative.

Example: Imagine a scene filled with suspense. Your voice lowers, your pace slows, and the words come out with measured intensity. This variation in delivery heightens the tension and keeps the listener on the edge of their seat.

✓ **Using Silence Effectively:** Silence is not the absence of communication, but a powerful tool in the hands of a skilled storyteller. Pauses can create anticipation, add emphasis to your words, and allow your listener to process the information you are sharing.

Example: Imagine a story filled with emotional moments. A well-placed pause after a climactic statement can magnify the impact, allowing the weight of the words to sink in and leaving a lasting impression on your listener.

Beyond Words:

While the power of storytelling lies primarily in the spoken word, non-verbal communication plays a vital role in its effectiveness. Gestures, facial expressions, and eye contact add layers of meaning and emotion to your narrative, enhancing its impact and drawing your listener deeper into the story.

Example: Imagine a storyteller using expressive hand gestures to paint a picture of a bustling marketplace. Their eyes sparkle with enthusiasm as they recount the sights and sounds, their voice rising and falling with the rhythm of the story. This non-verbal communication adds depth and dimension to the narrative, making it come alive for the listener.

The Power of Storytelling:

Mastering the art of storytelling is a transformative skill that transcends the spoken word. It allows you to:

✓ **Connect with others on a deeper level:** Stories create bridges between individuals, fostering empathy, understanding, and genuine connection.

✓ **Share your experiences and perspectives:** By weaving your personal narratives into conversations, you offer others a glimpse into your world, fostering deeper understanding and appreciation.

✓ **Leave a lasting impression:** Well-told stories resonate with listeners long after the last word is spoken. They leave a mark on their hearts and minds, inspiring reflection and influencing their thoughts and actions.

Conclusion:

Stories are not mere words. They are powerful tools for communication, connection, and transformation. By mastering the art of storytelling, you unlock the potential to captivate your audience, build meaningful relationships, and leave a lasting impact on the world. So, embrace the power of storytelling, weave your tales with passion and authenticity, and watch as you connect with others on a deeper level and create memories that will last a lifetime.

CHAPTER 13: Conversations on Difficult Topics

The art of conversation takes on a whole new meaning when it ventures beyond the realm of pleasantries and into the depths of challenging, complex, and even contentious topics. These conversations, while often fraught with emotional tension and differing viewpoints, offer a unique opportunity for profound understanding, personal growth, and the strengthening of relationships. However, navigating these waters effectively requires a delicate blend of courage, compassion, and communication skills.

Preparation and Planning:

Before embarking on a conversation that you anticipate might be difficult, it's crucial to prepare yourself mentally and emotionally. This involves the following steps:

1) **Identify your purpose and desired outcome:**

    What do you hope to achieve through this conversation? Are you seeking to:

    ✓ Educate the other person on a particular topic?
    ✓ Persuade them to adopt your perspective?
    ✓ Find common ground and build understanding?
    ✓ Offer support or simply listen without judgment?
    ✓ Resolve a conflict or issue?

    Having a clear aim will guide your approach, ensure you stay focused, and prevent the discussion from straying off course.

67

2) **Examine your own biases and assumptions:**

   ✓ Take an honest look at your preconceived notions and beliefs related to the topic. Do you hold any hidden biases or assumptions that might influence your perspective?

   ✓ Being aware of your own biases is crucial for approaching the conversation with an open mind and avoiding making unfair judgments about the other person's views.

3) **Gather knowledge and information:**

   ✓ Equip yourself with relevant facts, statistics, and research to support your arguments or questions. This will enhance your credibility, strengthen your position, and enable you to address any counterarguments effectively.

   ✓ Consider the different perspectives on the topic and familiarize yourself with the arguments opposing your own. This will help you anticipate potential challenges and formulate rebuttals in a respectful and informed manner.

4) **Practice active listening and empathy:**

   ✓ Rehearse how you will listen attentively to the other person's perspective without judgment or interruption. This involves giving them your full attention, making eye contact, and nodding to show you're engaged.

   ✓ Cultivate empathy by actively trying to understand their emotions, experiences, and the logic behind their viewpoint. This fosters trust and creates a safe space for open communication.

Initiating the Conversation:

Choosing the right time and setting is crucial for having a productive conversation on a difficult topic. Consider the following:

✓ **Timing:** Choose a time when both you and the other person are relaxed, unstressed, and have ample time to engage in a meaningful conversation.

68

Avoid initiating the conversation when they are tired, rushed, or in a bad mood.

✓ **Setting:** Select a private space where you can speak openly and honestly without distractions or interruptions. This could be a quiet room in your home, a private table at a café, or a walk in a peaceful park.

✓ **Approach:** Begin the conversation calmly and respectfully. Avoid making accusatory or inflammatory statements, and instead, focus on stating your intention for engaging in this discussion and expressing your willingness to hear their perspective.

Maintaining a Constructive Dialogue:

Remember, the goal of a difficult conversation is not necessarily to win an argument or force the other person to agree with your viewpoint. Rather, it's about fostering understanding, building connection, and finding common ground. Here are some key principles to keep in mind during the dialogue:

1) **Embrace open-ended questions:**

Instead of asking yes/no questions that limit the conversation, ask open-ended questions that encourage elaboration and understanding. Examples include:

   ✓ "How does this issue make you feel?"
   ✓ "What are your thoughts on this particular aspect of the problem?"
   ✓ "Can you explain your reasoning behind that statement?"
   ✓ "What are some potential solutions you see to this situation?"

Open-ended questions allow you to delve deeper into the other person's thought process, uncover their motivations, and identify areas of agreement or disagreement.

2) **Actively listen and acknowledge:**

Pay close attention to the other person's words, emotions, and non-verbal cues. Acknowledge their points, even if you disagree, to demonstrate respect and encourage further dialogue. Examples of acknowledging statements include:

69

- ✓ "I understand what you're saying, and I appreciate you sharing your perspective."
- ✓ "It sounds like this issue has caused you significant frustration."
- ✓ "I can see how you arrived at that conclusion based on your experience."
- ✓ "I hadn't considered that perspective before, thank you for sharing it."

By taking the time to truly listen and acknowledge their thoughts and feelings, you create a safe space for open communication and build trust in the relationship.

3) **Use "I" statements:**

Instead of making accusatory statements like "You always…" or "You never…" which can put the other person on the defensive, focus on sharing your own feelings and experiences using "I" statements. Examples include:

- ✓ "I feel frustrated when…"
- ✓ "I'm concerned about…"
- ✓ "I'm disappointed that…"
- ✓ "I would appreciate it if…"

By framing your concerns and observations in terms of your own feelings, you take responsibility for your own emotions and avoid blaming the other person. This reduces the risk of triggering defensiveness and encourages a more productive dialogue.

4) **Avoid interrupting and allow space for silence:**

Give the other person ample time to express themselves without interrupting or finishing their sentences. This demonstrates respect and allows them to fully articulate their thoughts and feelings.

Silence can also be a powerful tool in conversation. It provides space for reflection, processing information, and formulating a thoughtful response. Don't feel pressured to fill every silence with talk.

5) **Focus on understanding, not winning:**

70

Approach the conversation with a genuine desire to understand the other person's perspective, even if you don't agree with it. This involves listening attentively, asking clarifying questions, and avoiding the temptation to interrupt or launch into your own arguments before they have finished speaking.

Remember, the goal is not to win an argument or prove your point, but rather to gain a deeper understanding of each other's viewpoints and perspectives. This can lead to greater mutual respect and appreciation, even if you remain at odds on the specific issue.

6) Show empathy and compassion:

Acknowledge the other person's emotions and validate their experiences. This can be as simple as saying:

- ✓ "I can see why you would feel that way."
- ✓ "That must have been difficult for you."
- ✓ "I'm sorry that you had to experience that."

By showing empathy and compassion, you create a safe space for vulnerability and deeper connection. This allows the conversation to move beyond the intellectual level and into the realm of genuine human connection.

Respecting Boundaries and Maintaining Calm:

It's important to remember that not all difficult conversations need to reach a definitive conclusion. There will be times when it's necessary to agree to disagree and respect the other person's right to their own opinion. Here are some tips for navigating these situations:

- ✓ **Recognize when to take a break:** If the conversation becomes heated or unproductive, take a break to cool down and revisit the discussion later. This allows both of you to regain your composure and approach the dialogue with renewed perspective.

71

✓ **Set boundaries:** If the other person becomes aggressive or disrespectful, it's okay to set boundaries and disengage from the conversation. You have the right to protect your own emotional well-being.

✓ **Seek additional support:** If you find yourself struggling to navigate a particularly difficult conversation, consider seeking support from a trusted friend, family member, therapist, or counselor. They can provide a safe space to talk through your feelings and develop strategies for managing the situation effectively.

Moving Forward:

After engaging in a challenging conversation, take time to reflect on the experience. Consider the following questions:

✓ What did you learn from the conversation?
✓ What could you have done differently?
✓ What are the next steps you need to take?
✓ How can you apply what you learned to future conversations?

By reflecting on your experiences, you can continuously refine your communication skills and become more adept at navigating challenging conversations with grace, empathy, and understanding. Remember, even the most difficult conversations can be catalysts for personal growth, stronger relationships, and a more connected world.

Additional Tools and Strategies:

Here are some additional tools and strategies you can utilize to enhance your approach to difficult conversations:

✓ **Utilize "we" statements:** When appropriate, use "we" statements to create a sense of shared responsibility and common ground. This can be helpful for fostering collaboration and finding solutions together.

✓ **Emphasize common values:** Identify underlying values you share with the other person, even if your viewpoints differ on the specific topic. This can help build trust and remind you of the shared humanity that connects you.

✓ **Focus on solutions:** If the conversation revolves around a problem, shift the focus towards finding solutions together, rather than dwelling solely on the disagreements. This can be a more productive and constructive way to move forward.

✓ **Acknowledge areas of agreement:** Look for points of consensus, even if minor, to build upon during the discussion. This can help create a sense of progress and encourage continued dialogue.

✓ **Utilize humor:** In appropriate situations, humor can lighten the mood and defuse tension. This can be helpful in facilitating further dialogue and preventing the conversation from becoming overly serious or combative. However, it's important to be mindful of the other person's feelings and avoid using humor that could be insensitive or offensive.

✓ **Employ active listening techniques:** Active listening skills like nodding, mirroring, and maintaining eye contact demonstrate your attentiveness and encourage the other person to continue sharing their thoughts and feelings.

✓ **Summarize and paraphrase:** Periodically summarize the key points of the conversation and paraphrase what you've heard to ensure you're understanding their perspective correctly. This demonstrates your attentiveness and helps prevent misunderstandings.

✓ **Be assertive, not aggressive:** When expressing your own opinions and concerns, do so assertively, not aggressively. This involves stating your position clearly and confidently, while remaining respectful of the other person's views.

✓ **Prepare for potential objections:** Anticipate potential objections or arguments the other person might raise and prepare your responses in advance. This can help you stay calm and collected during the conversation and ensure you're able to address their concerns effectively.

✓ **Focus on the present:** Avoid bringing up past grievances or unrelated issues that could derail the current conversation. Instead, focus on the present issue and strive to resolve it constructively.

✓ **Remember, communication is a two-way street:** While your communication style and approach are important, remember that the

73

conversation's success depends on both parties actively engaging and participating. Be open to listening and learning from the other person's perspective, even if it differs from your own.

Conclusion:

Engaging in difficult conversations requires courage, skill, and empathy. By incorporating the principles outlined in this chapter, you can equip yourself with the tools and strategies necessary to navigate these challenging dialogues effectively. Remember, the goal is not always to reach a definitive agreement, but rather to foster understanding, build connection, and explore different perspectives. By approaching these conversations with an open mind, a respectful demeanor, and a genuine desire to learn and connect, you can contribute to creating a world where communication is not a source of conflict, but a catalyst for growth and understanding.

CHAPTER 14: Handling Silences and Awkward Moments

Even the most seasoned conversationalists encounter the dreaded silence – that unwelcome guest that crashes the party, leaving everyone staring at their shoes in awkward anticipation. But fear not, fellow conversationalists, for silence is not a foe, but a tool. Learn to wield it with grace, and watch your conversations blossom.

Understanding the Nature of Silence:

Silences occur for various reasons, each offering valuable insights into the conversation's flow. Let's delve deeper:

- ✓ **Reflection Pitstops:** Sometimes, a pause allows for deeper processing. Imagine discussing a personal experience; silence grants you crucial moments to gather your thoughts and craft a heartfelt response.

- ✓ **Gear-Shifting Moments:** Conversations are dynamic, flitting between topics like butterflies on a breeze. Silence acts as a natural transition, a pause before diving into a new topic with renewed interest.

- ✓ **Comfort in the Quiet:** Introverts often find solace in silence, a haven from the constant barrage of words. Respect their need for quietude and allow the conversation to unfold at their own pace.

- ✓ **Awkwardness Unveiled:** Sometimes, silence betrays discomfort or uncertainty. A shy individual might clam up, unsure of how to proceed. Recognizing these cues allows you to offer gentle support and guide the conversation back on track.

Embracing the Pause:

Instead of scrambling to fill the void, embrace silence as a natural part of the conversation. Embrace the opportunity to:

- ✓ **Reflect and Respond:** Contemplate what has been said and formulate your response. Consider the other person's perspective and craft a thoughtful reply.

- ✓ **Become a Keen Observer:** Watch the other person's non-verbal cues. A furrowed brow might indicate confusion, while a relaxed smile suggests comfort. Let these subtle gestures guide your next move.

- ✓ **Find Inner Peace:** Take a few deep breaths and relax. Allow yourself to be comfortable in the quiet, without the pressure to perform.

When to Break the Silence:

While silence holds value, knowing when to step in is crucial. Consider these cues:

- ✓ **Uncomfortable Silence:** If the silence stretches on, causing discomfort for yourself or the other person, gently nudge the conversation forward. Ask a question related to the previous topic or make a lighthearted observation.

- ✓ **Bridging the Gap:** Transitioning between topics can be tricky. Use a well-timed silence to mark the end of one subject and introduce the next naturally.

- ✓ **Sharing with Relevance:** If a thought strikes you, connected to the current discussion, share it during a natural pause. Your contribution might spark a lively exchange of ideas.

Filling the Void Gracefully:

When the time comes to break the silence, do so with intention. Here are some strategies:

- ✓ **Open-Ended Inquiry:** Ask open-ended questions that invite elaboration, drawing the other person into the conversation. Instead of "Did you enjoy the movie?", inquire, "What did you think of the movie's ending?"

76

- ✓ **Observations with a Twist:** Observe your surroundings or the conversation itself, adding a unique perspective. For example, "The rain outside sounds just like the music we were listening to earlier, don't you think?"

- ✓ **Sharing Stories:** A personal anecdote can add a touch of humor or vulnerability, forging a deeper connection. Relate a similar experience, adding a new dimension to the conversation.

- ✓ **Humor as a Bridge:** Laughter can break the tension and lighten the mood. However, ensure your humor is appropriate and doesn't offend the other person.

- ✓ **Acknowledging the Silence:** Sometimes, simply acknowledging the elephant in the room can be enough. A playful, "Well, this is an interesting silence!" can break the ice and invite further dialogue.

Remember:

- ✓ **Natural Flow is Key:** Don't force the conversation. If it feels unnatural, allow the silence to linger. A genuine interaction is worth more than strained words.

- ✓ **Body Language Matters:** Maintain eye contact, smile naturally, and have an open posture. These nonverbal cues convey confidence and encourage the other person to engage.

- ✓ **Focus on the Other Person:** Pay attention to their responses, both verbal and nonverbal. Respond accordingly, ensuring your communication is truly a two-way street.

Turning Awkwardness into a Bond:

Awkwardness, though uncomfortable, can be a catalyst for connection and intimacy. Here's how to transform it into an opportunity:

- ✓ **Embrace the Awkwardness:** Acknowledge the awkwardness with a smile or a lighthearted comment. This can break the tension and create a sense of shared experience.

- ✓ **Humor to the Rescue:** A well-timed joke can disarm awkwardness and foster a sense of ease. However, avoid humor that belittles or mocks the other person.

- ✓ **Vulnerability Breeds Connection:** Sharing your own awkward moments can make the other person feel more comfortable and open up. It demonstrates your humanity and authenticity, paving the way for deeper connection.

- ✓ **Shifting Perspectives:** Sometimes, reframing the awkwardness can shift your perspective. Instead of seeing it as a negative experience, view it as a chance to build trust and intimacy. This shift in mindset can make the situation feel less daunting.

- ✓ **Finding Common Ground:** Awkwardness often arises from feeling different or misunderstood. Use this opportunity to find common ground with the other person. Share similar experiences, interests, or feelings to bridge the gap and create a sense of belonging.

- ✓ **Growth through Discomfort:** Stepping outside your comfort zone can be challenging, but it's also a powerful catalyst for growth. Embrace the discomfort of awkwardness as an opportunity to learn about yourself and improve your communication skills.

- ✓ **Remembering the Bigger Picture:** Keep in mind that awkwardness is a fleeting experience. It doesn't define you or the relationship. Focus on the positive aspects of the interaction and let go of any anxieties or negative thoughts.

- ✓ **Embrace the Journey:** Conversations are dynamic journeys, filled with twists, turns, and unexpected pauses. Embrace the silence, the awkward moments, and the unexpected turns as valuable parts of the journey. Remember, the most meaningful conversations often arise from the spaces in between the words.

By learning to navigate silence and awkwardness with grace and understanding, you can transform them from obstacles to opportunities for deeper connection, self-discovery, and richer conversations. So, relax, embrace the silence, and let the

78

conversations flow freely. You might be surprised at the beauty and connection that awaits you just beyond the awkward pause.

Examples of Handling Silences and Awkward Moments

Let's explore some concrete examples of how to handle different types of silence and awkwardness:

✓ **Scenario 1: The First Date Silence**

You're having dinner with someone you're interested in, but there's an uncomfortable silence stretching between you like an abyss. Instead of panicking, take a deep breath and apply some of the strategies we discussed.

Solution: Ask an open-ended question about their interests or hobbies. For example, "What's one thing you're passionate about in life?" This invites them to share their thoughts and potentially spark a lively conversation. Alternatively, you could share a relevant observation about the restaurant or the surrounding environment. "This place has a really cool vibe, don't you think?" can be a springboard for further discussion. If all else fails, acknowledge the silence with a lighthearted comment like, "Well, this is an interesting silence!" and laugh it off together.

✓ **Scenario 2: The Job Interview Silence**

You're midway through a job interview, and a question leaves you feeling slightly unsure of how to respond. The silence feels heavy with anticipation.

Solution: Take a moment to collect your thoughts and formulate your answer. Avoid filling the silence with nervous rambling or apologies. Instead, rephrase the question in your mind to clarify its meaning. If necessary, ask for clarification or rephrase the question to ensure you understand it correctly. This demonstrates your thoughtfulness and composure. Once you are ready, deliver your response with confidence and clarity.

✓ **Scenario 3: The Family Dinner Awkwardness**

You're having dinner with your extended family, and a sensitive topic arises, causing tension and awkwardness.

79

Solution: Acknowledge the discomfort without escalating the situation. You could say something like, "It seems like this topic is causing some tension. Perhaps we can table it for now and come back to it later when everyone has had a chance to cool down." This shows your emotional intelligence and ability to navigate difficult situations. Alternatively, you could try to redirect the conversation to a more positive topic that everyone can enjoy.

✓ **Scenario 4: The Online Dating Chat Silence**

You're chatting with someone interesting online, but the conversation seems to have stalled, leaving you feeling uncertain about how to proceed.

Solution: Instead of giving up, try sending them a thoughtful message related to something they've shared in their profile. This shows you've been paying attention and are genuinely interested in getting to know them better. For example, if they mentioned their love for travel, you could ask them about their dream destination and why it holds such significance. Remember to be genuine and ask questions that encourage open-ended responses.

Remember: There's no one-size-fits-all solution to handling silence and awkwardness. The key is to be adaptable, resourceful, and most importantly, yourself. By approaching each situation with a positive and open-minded attitude, you'll be well on your way to mastering the art of conversation and forging meaningful connections with others.

Beyond the Basics: Advanced Techniques for Navigating Silence and Awkwardness

While the strategies mentioned earlier provide a solid foundation, mastering the art of navigating silence and awkwardness requires venturing beyond the basics. Here are some advanced techniques to consider:

1) **Active Listening to the Unspoken:**

   Silence doesn't always demand immediate response. Pay close attention to non-verbal cues like body language, facial expressions, and tone of voice. These often convey unspoken emotions and intentions, offering valuable insights into the conversation's subtext.

2) **Embrace the Power of "Hmm" and "Ah":**

80

Simple interjections like "Hmm" and "Ah" can hold immense power in conversation. They acknowledge the other person's words, encourage further elaboration, and buy you time to formulate a thoughtful response.

3) **Master the Art of the Pause:**

Don't rush to fill every silence. Learn to leverage the power of pause. It adds weight to your words, allows for deeper reflection, and creates anticipation for what you have to say next.

4) **Explore the World of Open-Ended Statements:**

Instead of asking yes-or-no questions, utilize open-ended statements that invite the other person to share their thoughts and feelings. For example, instead of saying, "Do you like this movie?", try saying, "What are your thoughts on the way the movie was filmed?"

5) **Be Comfortable with Uncomfortable Topics:**

Difficult conversations are inevitable. Practice navigating them with grace and sensitivity. Acknowledge the discomfort, express empathy, and focus on finding common ground instead of escalating the situation.

6) **Turn Silence into a Collaborative Experience:**

Instead of seeing silence as a void to be filled, view it as a space for co-creation. Invite the other person to share their thoughts, ideas, and feelings. This collaborative approach fosters deeper connection and understanding.

7) **Practice Self-Awareness:**

Understanding your own triggers and anxieties surrounding silence and awkwardness is crucial. This allows you to manage them effectively and respond in a calm and collected manner.

8) **Celebrate the Beauty of Imperfection:**

Remember, nobody is perfect. Even the most skilled conversationalists experience silence and awkwardness. Don't strive for flawlessness. Embrace the imperfection and allow your genuine self to shine through.

81

9) **Cultivate a Growth Mindset:**

View each awkward moment as an opportunity to learn and grow. Analyze what worked, what didn't, and adjust your approach accordingly. This continuous learning process will elevate your communication skills to new heights.

10) **Enjoy the Journey:**

Conversation is a journey, not a **destination.** Embrace the twists, turns, and occasional awkward silences as part of the adventure. Focus on connecting with the other person, enjoying the present moment, and allowing the conversation to unfold naturally.

By mastering these advanced techniques, you'll transform silence and awkwardness from dreaded foes into valuable allies. You'll become a more confident, compassionate, and effective communicator, building stronger connections and enriching your life in the process. Remember, silence is not the enemy of conversation; it's the space where true connection can bloom.

Conclusion

Silence is an integral part of any meaningful conversation. It allows for reflection, fosters deeper understanding, and creates space for genuine connection. By learning to embrace silence and navigate awkwardness with grace, you unlock the true potential of conversation.

Imagine a conversation as a symphony. The words are the notes, rich and varied, each carrying its own melody. But without the pauses, the rests, the moments of silence, the symphony would be a cacophony, devoid of meaning and beauty. It is in the silence between the notes that we truly understand the music.

Similarly, in conversation, silence allows the words to resonate, to linger in the air, and to evoke deeper emotions. It is the space where meaning is constructed, where understanding blossoms, and where connection thrives.

So, the next time you find yourself facing silence in a conversation, don't panic. Don't rush to fill the void with meaningless chatter. Instead, embrace it. See it as an opportunity to connect with your inner self and the person across from you. Listen

82

to the unspoken words, the subtle cues, and the emotions that lie beneath the surface.

By learning to dance with silence, you'll transform your conversations from mere exchanges of words into profound experiences of connection, shared meaning, and lasting impact. Remember, the most beautiful music is often born from the quiet spaces between the notes.

83

CHAPTER 15: Conflict Resolution in Conversations

The tapestry of conversation, even the most vibrant and engaging, is not woven without threads of conflict. Disagreements, misunderstandings, and opposing viewpoints inevitably arise, and it is in the crucible of such clashes that our true communication skills are forged. This chapter delves into the art of conflict resolution in conversations, equipping you with the tools and techniques to transform potential clashes into opportunities for deeper understanding and more resilient relationships.

Delving Deeper: Understanding the Source of Conflict

The journey towards effective conflict resolution begins with an exploration of its root cause. Is it a clash of values, a genuine difference of opinion, or simply a misunderstanding of information? Identifying the underlying issue is akin to uncovering a hidden map, allowing us to navigate the conversation with greater clarity and purpose.

For instance, imagine a conversation with a close friend about your differing political views. Instead of attributing their stance to mere ignorance, you might discover a deep-seated concern for social justice that fuels their perspective. This newfound understanding serves as a bridge, allowing you to engage in a more meaningful dialogue and explore the roots of your disagreement without resorting to unproductive defensiveness or personal attacks.

Active Listening and Empathy: The Cornerstones of Resolution

84

As previously discussed in Chapter 5, active listening remains the cornerstone of navigating conflict. By truly hearing and understanding the other person's perspective, we create a safe space for resolution and compromise. This involves not just listening to their words, but also paying close attention to their body language, tone of voice, and underlying emotions.

Empathy, the ability to see things from their point of view, plays a crucial role in fostering a sense of connection and understanding. Imagine a conversation with your partner about their workload, where instead of dismissing their stress as trivial, you attempt to see the situation through their eyes, acknowledging the pressure and challenges they face. This empathetic approach paves the way for deeper communication and collaborative problem-solving.

"I" Statements: Disarming Defensiveness and Fostering Connection

Instead of pointing accusatory fingers and hurling "you" statements, which often ignite defensiveness and escalate the situation, consider using "I" statements to express your feelings and concerns. This approach takes ownership of your experience and fosters a more constructive dialogue.

For example, in a conversation with your colleague about their tendency to interrupt, instead of saying "You always interrupt me!" which is likely to trigger a defensive reaction, try "I feel frustrated when I'm interrupted because I want to be able to fully share my thoughts." This shift in perspective places the focus on your experience and opens the door for a more productive discussion about finding solutions that respect both of your needs.

From Differences to Common Ground: Finding Shared Values

Even amidst a seemingly insurmountable conflict, there are likely underlying values or goals that you and the other person share. Identifying these commonalities is akin to discovering a hidden treasure, providing a foundation for building bridges and forging solutions that strengthen the relationship.

Imagine a disagreement with your family member about their parenting style. Despite the differing approaches, you might discover a shared commitment to raising kind, compassionate, and responsible children. This common ground can serve as a starting point for finding solutions that honor both of your perspectives while ensuring the well-being of the child.

Communication Techniques for De-escalation and Resolution

85

✓ **Clarification:** Ask clarifying questions to ensure you fully understand the other person's perspective. This helps avoid misunderstandings and opens the door for further communication. For example, "What exactly did you mean when you said that?" or "Could you elaborate on your point?" demonstrate your genuine interest in understanding their position.

✓ **Paraphrasing:** Reflect back what you heard to confirm understanding and show that you are actively listening. This demonstrates respect and encourages further communication. For example, "So, you're feeling frustrated because you feel like you're not being heard?" allows the other person to confirm or correct your understanding.

✓ **Validation:** Acknowledge the other person's feelings, even if you disagree with their point of view. This creates a safe space for open and honest communication. Saying "I understand that you're feeling hurt by my words" shows empathy and can help de-escalate the situation.

✓ **Giving and Receiving Feedback:** Offer constructive criticism in a respectful and solution-oriented manner. Be open to receiving feedback as well, and approach it as an opportunity for growth and improvement. For example, "I would appreciate it if you could avoid interrupting me so that I can finish my thoughts" provides specific feedback without resorting to personal attacks.

✓ **De-escalation and Timeouts:** Saying "I need a moment to gather my thoughts" or "Perhaps we should revisit this conversation later when we're both feeling calmer" can be crucial in preventing the situation from escalating further.

Compromise and Win-Win Solutions: Finding Common Ground

Instead of approaching conflict as a zero-sum game where one person wins and the other loses, focus on seeking solutions that benefit all parties involved. This requires creativity, open-mindedness, and a willingness to compromise. Brainstorming various solutions and exploring different perspectives can lead to "win-win" outcomes that strengthen the relationship and foster a sense of shared success.

For example, imagine a disagreement with your roommate about noise levels in your shared apartment. Instead of each person stubbornly defending their preferences,

86

you might explore solutions like setting quiet hours, investing in noise-canceling headphones, or creating designated areas for relaxation and concentration. This collaborative approach allows both of you to get your needs met without resorting to ultimatums or resentment.

Seeking Professional Help: When Additional Support is Needed

There are situations where the conflict is particularly complex or involves underlying personal issues that require additional support. In these instances, seeking professional help from a therapist or counselor can be invaluable. They can provide a neutral and objective perspective, offer guidance on communication techniques, and help you develop healthier patterns of interaction.

For instance, imagine a long-standing conflict with a family member that seems to stem from unresolved past issues. A therapist can facilitate a safe and supportive environment for exploring these issues, fostering deeper understanding, and finding ways to move forward in a healthy and positive manner.

Remember:

- ✓ Conflict is an inevitable, and often necessary, part of any relationship.

- ✓ Approach conflict as an opportunity for learning and growth, not just a source of frustration.

- ✓ Focus on understanding the other person's perspective and fostering empathy.

- ✓ Communicate assertively and respectfully, using "I" statements and avoiding accusatory language.

- ✓ Be open to compromise and seek win-win solutions.

- ✓ Don't be afraid to seek professional help if needed.

By implementing these strategies and cultivating a mindful and compassionate approach, you can transform conflict from a source of discord into a catalyst for deeper understanding, stronger relationships, and ultimately, a more fulfilling life. The tapestry of conversation, once woven with threads of conflict, can become a

87

work of art, vibrant with the richness of diverse perspectives and strengthened by the resilience of human connection.

Beyond Words: The Role of Non-Verbal Communication

While words form the bedrock of communication, the non-verbal cues we transmit play a crucial role in forging connection and understanding, particularly during conflict. Our body language, facial expressions, and tone of voice can either amplify our words and foster understanding or contradict them, creating confusion and discord.

Imagine a conversation with a friend where you're discussing a sensitive topic. Although your tone is calm and collected, your crossed arms and furrowed brow might convey defensiveness and closed-mindedness, unknowingly pushing your friend away. Conversely, maintaining open posture, making direct eye contact, and mirroring their expressions can signal receptivity and encourage open communication.

Understanding the Power of Silence

Silence, often regarded as an awkward void in conversation, can be a powerful tool in conflict resolution. It allows for reflection, processing of information, and de-escalation of emotions. Taking a moment of silence before responding can help you gather your thoughts and formulate a more thoughtful and constructive response.

For example, imagine a heated discussion with your partner about finances. Taking a pause before responding, instead of immediately reacting with your own argument, can create space for understanding and compromise. This silence can be filled with reflection on their perspective and a conscious effort to choose your words carefully, fostering a more productive dialogue.

Developing Emotional Intelligence

Emotional intelligence, the ability to understand and manage your own emotions and those of others, plays a vital role in navigating conflict effectively. Recognizing your own triggers and learning to regulate them prevents emotional outbursts that can escalate the situation. Similarly, being attuned to the other person's emotions allows you to respond with empathy and understanding.

Imagine a conversation with a colleague who is visibly upset about a missed deadline. Employing emotional intelligence involves acknowledging their frustration without

88

being reactive, perhaps by saying "I understand that you're feeling frustrated about this situation." This approach demonstrates empathy and creates an environment where the issue can be addressed calmly and collaboratively.

Cultivating Forgiveness and Letting Go

Holding onto resentment and anger in the aftermath of conflict can prevent healing and foster further discord. Forgiveness, however, is not about condoning the other person's actions but rather choosing to release your own emotional attachments to the situation. This allows you to move forward with a clearer and calmer perspective.

For example, imagine having a heated argument with a family member. While it may be challenging to forget the hurtful words exchanged, practicing forgiveness allows you to let go of the negativity and focus on rebuilding the relationship. This might involve offering a sincere apology, acknowledging your own contribution to the conflict, and actively working towards reconciliation.

The Ripple Effect of Effective Conflict Resolution

The positive impact of effective conflict resolution extends far beyond the immediate resolution of the issue at hand. By demonstrating respect, empathy, and a willingness to compromise, you create a ripple effect that strengthens relationships, fosters trust, and builds a foundation for deeper understanding and connection.

Imagine a workplace where colleagues are comfortable voicing their opinions and knowing that they will be heard and respected, even if they disagree. This open and collaborative environment fosters innovation, problem-solving, and ultimately, organizational success.

Conclusion

Conflict resolution is not a finite skill mastered once and applied ever after. It is a lifelong journey of learning, self-reflection, and continuous improvement. By incorporating the strategies discussed in this chapter, you can navigate the inevitable clashes of conversation with grace, resilience, and a commitment to understanding and connection. Remember, the art of conversation is not about avoiding conflict, but about transforming it into an opportunity for growth, strengthening relationships, and ultimately, enriching your life.

89

CHAPTER 16: The Art of Ending Conversations

Just like a virtuoso's final flourish on a grand piano, the closing act of a conversation can resonate long after the last word is spoken. Mastering the art of ending well is an often overlooked, yet crucial skill that can elevate your communication effectiveness and leave a lasting positive impression. This chapter delves into the intricacies of crafting satisfying closures, ensuring everyone involved feels heard, respected, and eager for future exchanges.

Recognizing the Closing Cue

Similar to a seasoned conductor anticipating the final note, recognizing the opportune moment to conclude a conversation is essential. This requires keen observation of both verbal and nonverbal cues:

Verbal Cues:

- ✓ **Conversational flow:** Does the energy naturally dissipate, with sentences tapering off and silences increasing in length?

- ✓ **Filler phrases:** Do phrases like "well," "anyway," or "so..." become more frequent, indicating a search for an exit point?

- ✓ **Time references:** Are mentions of time constraints, appointments, or deadlines subtly woven into the conversation?

- ✓ **Shifting focus:** Does the conversation veer off topic repeatedly, suggesting waning interest in the current discussion?

90

Nonverbal Cues:

- ✓ **Restless body language:** Are people fidgeting, shifting their weight, or glancing at their watches, indicating a desire to move on?

- ✓ **Decreased eye contact:** Does eye contact become less frequent or more fleeting, suggesting dwindling engagement?

- ✓ **Closed postures:** Are arms crossed or shoulders hunched, signifying a desire to withdraw from the conversation?

- ✓ **Facial expressions:** Do expressions convey boredom, fatigue, or impatience, hinting at a readiness to end the interaction?

By paying close attention to these signals, you can discern the most appropriate moment to initiate the closing, ensuring a smooth and natural transition.

Crafting the Perfect Closing Act

Like a skilled sculptor meticulously shaping a masterpiece, the art of ending conversations requires careful consideration and nuanced execution. Here are several strategies to master the closing act, depending on the context and desired outcome:

1) **The Artful Recap and Gratitude:**

   - ✓ **Summarize key points:** Briefly recap the main takeaways from the conversation, demonstrating attentiveness and solidifying the knowledge exchanged.

   - ✓ **Express appreciation:** Thank the other person for their insights, time, or contribution, reinforcing the value of the interaction.

     Example: "It was fascinating learning about your experience with [topic]. Thank you for sharing your unique perspective."

2) **Seizing the Opportunity for Action:**

91

✓ **Convert conversation into action:** If the discussion sparks an idea or next step, propose a concrete action plan. This creates a sense of closure and momentum.

✓ **Connect for future collaboration:** Suggest a follow-up meeting, exchange contact information, or propose a collaborative project. This fosters long-term connections and keeps the conversation alive.

Example: "This conversation has inspired me to [action]. Perhaps we could schedule a meeting to discuss it further?"

3) **Introducing a Natural Pause:**

✓ **Acknowledge the interruption:** If you need to leave mid-conversation, express your regret and suggest resuming later.

✓ **Offer a timeframe for continuation:** Suggest a specific time or context for revisiting the conversation, demonstrating genuine interest in continuing the dialogue.

Example: "Unfortunately, I need to head off now. Would you be available to continue this conversation next week over coffee?"

4) **Utilizing External Cues:**

✓ **Leverage external circumstances:** Use environmental factors like impending rain, a nearby acquaintance, or a time constraint as a natural closing point.

✓ **Express gratitude for the interaction:** Acknowledge the time spent together and offer a sincere farewell.

Example: "It looks like bad weather is rolling in. It was a pleasure chatting with you. Take care and be well."

5) **The Open-Ended Farewell:**

✓ **Express desire for future interactions:** Leave the door open for future conversations, demonstrating your interest in maintaining the connection.

92

- ✓ **Offer a warm and friendly farewell:** Use phrases like "I look forward to seeing you again soon" or "It was lovely meeting you," conveying a positive and welcoming tone.

  Example: "I've enjoyed getting to know you today. I look forward to connecting again soon."

6) **The Simple and Sincere:**

  - ✓ **Direct and genuine farewell:** In casual settings, a straightforward, heartfelt "It was great chatting with you!" can suffice.

  - ✓ **Maintain eye contact and smile:** Nonverbal cues play a crucial role in conveying sincerity and warmth.

    Example: "Well, I have to get going, but it was great talking to you. Take it easy!"

Remember, the key to a successful closing lies in genuineness and respect. Maintain eye contact, offer a warm smile, and express genuine appreciation for the interaction. These seemingly small gestures can have a significant impact on the lasting impression you leave.

Avoiding Common Mishaps

Even the most seasoned conversationalist can stumble during the closing act. Be mindful of these common pitfalls to avoid undermining your efforts:

1) **The Disappearing Act:**

  - ✓ **Abrupt departure:** Vanishing abruptly without explanation can leave the other person feeling confused, disrespected, and wondering if they offended you.

  - ✓ **No closure or explanation:** Offering a brief explanation for your departure, even if it's just "I need to run," provides closure and prevents misunderstandings.

2) **Monopolizing the Closing:**

93

- ✓ **Dominating the conversation:** The closing shouldn't be a one-man show. Allow the other person to share their thoughts and feelings, ensuring a balanced and inclusive exchange.

- ✓ **Focusing only on yourself:** Avoid ending the conversation by talking about your own plans or obligations. Ensure the focus remains on expressing gratitude and acknowledging the other person's time.

3) **Negativity at the Finale:**

- ✓ **Ending on a sour note:** Avoid ending the conversation with negative comments, criticisms, or complaints. This can leave a bad taste in the other person's mouth and undermine the positive aspects of the interaction.

- ✓ **Focus on the positive:** Even if the conversation wasn't entirely successful, highlight the positive aspects and express appreciation for the other person's contribution.

4) **Excessive Apologies:**

- ✓ **Over-apologizing for leaving:** Apologizing profusely for ending the conversation can come across as insincere or imply that you've done something wrong.

- ✓ **Confident and genuine farewell:** Unless you've genuinely caused an inconvenience, a simple, confident "It was great chatting with you" suffices.

5) **Failing to Follow Through:**

- ✓ **Promises left unfulfilled:** If you promised to follow up on something, ensure you do it promptly. Failing to keep your word undermines trust and makes it difficult to maintain a positive connection.

- ✓ **Demonstrate reliability and commitment:** Following through on your commitments shows that you value the relationship and are reliable, fostering trust and respect.

94

6) **The Inconsiderate Rush:**

   ✓ **Ignoring the other person's time constraints:** Be mindful of the other person's schedule and avoid dragging out the conversation if they appear pressed for time.

   ✓ **Respecting time boundaries:** Pay attention to verbal and nonverbal cues indicating the other person needs to leave, and graciously end the conversation.

By avoiding these common pitfalls, you can ensure that your conversations end on a positive note, leaving a lasting impression of respect, consideration, and genuine interest.

Remember, the art of ending well is not about mastering a formula, but rather about being mindful, respectful, and genuine. By incorporating these principles into your interactions, you can elevate your communication skills, strengthen your relationships, and ensure that every conversation leaves a positive and lasting impression.

Beyond the Closing Act: The Power of Lasting Impressions

While the final words spoken undoubtedly hold weight, the true impact of a conversation extends far beyond the closing act. The lasting impression you leave hinges on the overall experience you create for the other person. Here's how to ensure your conversations resonate long after the final goodbye:

1) **Cultivating Genuine Interest:**

   ✓ **Active listening:** Go beyond simply hearing words and actively listen to understand the other person's thoughts, feelings, and perspectives.

   ✓ **Asking insightful questions:** Demonstrate your interest by asking thoughtful questions that encourage deeper engagement and meaningful dialogue.

   ✓ **Being present in the moment:** Avoid distractions and focus fully on the conversation, conveying your genuine interest and respect.

2) **Fostering a Positive Atmosphere:**

95

✓ **Smiling warmly and maintaining eye contact:** Nonverbal cues play a crucial role in creating a welcoming and safe space for open communication.

✓ **Using positive body language:** Leaning in, nodding your head, and maintaining an open posture signal engagement and attentiveness.

✓ **Offering sincere compliments:** Recognizing and acknowledging the other person's contributions creates a positive atmosphere and fosters mutual respect.

3) **Remembering the Little Things:**

✓ **Following up on promises:** Keeping your word builds trust and demonstrates your commitment to the relationship.

✓ **Remembering details:** Taking note of personal details, like someone's upcoming trip or a recent achievement, shows you care and are genuinely interested.

✓ **Sending a thoughtful note or message:** After a particularly meaningful conversation, a brief thank-you note or message can solidify the positive connection.

4) **Creating Shared Experiences:**

✓ **Finding common interests:** Discovering shared passions or experiences strengthens the bond and provides a foundation for future interactions.

✓ **Engaging in collaborative activities:** Working together on a project or activity creates shared memories and reinforces the connection.

✓ **Offering genuine support:** When someone faces a challenge or celebrates a success, offer your support and encouragement, demonstrating your empathy and care.

5) **Leaving a Legacy of Learning:**

96

✓ **Sharing your knowledge and expertise:** If you possess knowledge or skills relevant to the other person's interests, offer to share them, fostering mutual growth and learning.

✓ **Inquiring about their insights:** Actively seek the other person's perspective, showing your willingness to learn and be open to new ideas.

✓ **Leaving them with something to ponder:** Share a thought-provoking quote, a challenging question, or a new perspective to encourage continued reflection and growth.

By incorporating these principles into your communication style, you can transform your conversations from fleeting interactions into impactful experiences that leave a lasting positive impression. Remember, the power of communication lies not only in the words spoken but also in the emotions evoked and the connections forged. Cultivate genuine interest, create a positive atmosphere, and leave a legacy of learning, and you'll find that your conversations become more than just exchanges of words; they become opportunities to connect with others on a deeper level, leaving an enduring mark on their hearts and minds.

The Ripple Effect: Expanding Your Conversational Impact

The art of ending conversations isn't simply about mastering the final moments; it's about understanding the ripple effect your interactions create. Your conversations have the potential to spark positive change, inspire others, and leave a lasting impact that extends far beyond the immediate exchange.

1) **Building a Community of Connection:**

✓ **Initiating meaningful conversations:** By actively engaging with others and fostering genuine connections, you contribute to a more positive and connected community.

✓ **Encouraging open dialogue:** Promote open and respectful dialogue on important issues, fostering understanding and collaboration.

✓ **Sharing your knowledge and experiences:** Offer your insights and expertise to help others learn and grow, creating a ripple effect of positive change.

97

2) **Empowering and Inspiring Others:**

  - ✓ **Providing encouragement and support:** Offer words of encouragement and support, helping others overcome challenges and reach their full potential.

  - ✓ **Sharing stories of resilience and success:** Inspiring others by sharing your own stories of overcoming obstacles and achieving goals.

  - ✓ **Being a positive role model:** Demonstrate positive communication skills, empathy, and respect, inspiring others to do the same.

3) **Sparking Creativity and Innovation:**

  - ✓ **Engaging in thought-provoking conversations:** Challenge existing perspectives and encourage creative thinking by discussing diverse viewpoints.

  - ✓ **Sharing new ideas and perspectives:** Introduce others to new information and broaden their horizons, sparking innovation and problem-solving.

  - ✓ **Creating a collaborative environment:** Foster an environment where ideas are shared freely and collaboratively, leading to groundbreaking solutions.

4) **Promoting Understanding and Empathy:**

  - ✓ **Actively listening to and understanding diverse perspectives:** Engaging in respectful dialogue with those who hold different viewpoints fosters understanding and acceptance.

  - ✓ **Empathizing with others' experiences:** Stepping into someone else's shoes and considering their feelings builds bridges and promotes compassion.

  - ✓ **Sharing your own experiences and vulnerabilities:** Opening up about your own experiences can build trust, encourage others to do the same, and deepen understanding.

5) **Leaving a Legacy of Positive Change:**

- ✓ **Taking action on your conversations:** Don't let your words be mere words; translate your conversations into concrete actions and initiatives that create positive change.

- ✓ **Motivating others to take action:** Inspire and empower others to contribute to causes they believe in, creating a ripple effect of positive impact.

- ✓ **Leaving the world a better place:** By engaging in meaningful conversations, fostering connections, and inspiring action, you can leave a legacy that makes a lasting difference.

Remember, every conversation is an opportunity to connect with others, share your unique perspective, and contribute to something larger than yourself. So, embrace the art of ending well, not just as a way to conclude an interaction, but as a way to ensure your conversations leave a positive and lasting impact on the world around you.

Embracing the Journey: Continuous Growth and Transformation

The art of ending conversations is not a static skill; it's a dynamic journey of continuous learning and growth. As you engage in more interactions, reflect on your experiences, and learn from both successes and stumbles, your ability to navigate the closing act will evolve and blossom.

1) **Reflection and Self-Evaluation:**

- ✓ **Take time to reflect on your conversations:** After each interaction, take a moment to reflect on what went well, what could have been improved, and what you learned.

- ✓ **Identify areas for improvement:** Be honest with yourself and identify areas where you can refine your closing skills.

- ✓ **Seek feedback from others:** Ask trusted friends, colleagues, or mentors for constructive feedback on your communication style.

2) **Continuous Learning and Growth:**

99

✓ **Observe and learn from others:** Pay attention to how skilled communicators navigate the closing act and incorporate their techniques into your own repertoire.

✓ **Seek out learning opportunities:** Enrol in workshops, attend seminars, or read books and articles on communication and conversation skills.

✓ **Embrace your mistakes:** Don't see mistakes as failures but as opportunities to learn and grow. View them as stepping stones on your journey to becoming a masterful conversationalist.

3) **Adapting to Different Contexts:**

✓ **Recognize the unique needs of each situation:** Be mindful of the context of the conversation and tailor your closing approach accordingly.

✓ **Adjust your style based on the audience:** Pay attention to the other person's communication style and adjust your approach to create a comfortable and engaging interaction.

✓ **Embrace the unexpected:** Be prepared for unexpected situations and develop the flexibility to adapt your closing style accordingly.

4) **Embracing Authenticity and Vulnerability:**

✓ **Strive to be genuine in your interactions:** Authenticity fosters trust and connection, making your closing words more impactful.

✓ **Don't be afraid to show your vulnerability:** Sharing your own feelings and experiences can create a deeper level of connection with the other person.

✓ **Be true to yourself:** Don't try to be someone you're not; embrace your unique personality and communication style.

5) **Celebrating the Journey:**

✓ **Take pride in your progress:** Acknowledge and celebrate your achievements in mastering the art of ending conversations.

100

✓ **Embrace the joy of connection:** Appreciate the power of conversation in building relationships and creating meaningful experiences.

✓ **Never stop learning and growing:** View your journey in mastering the art of ending conversations as an ongoing process of exploration and discovery.

By embracing reflection, continuous learning, adaptability, authenticity, and celebration, you can transform the art of ending conversations from a mere skill into a powerful tool for connecting with others, creating positive impact, and leaving a lasting legacy of warmth, respect, and meaningful interaction. Remember, the journey is just as important as the destination. So, enjoy the process of learning and growing, and allow yourself to be transformed by the power of conversation.

Conclusion

As you close the book on this exploration of conversation endings, remember that the art lies not in rigidly following a script, but in cultivating a genuine connection that transcends the words spoken. It's about recognizing the nuances of human interaction, adapting to the ever-changing flow of conversation, and leaving a lasting impression that resonates long after the final goodbye.

Ultimately, mastering the art of ending conversations is about more than crafting the perfect closing line. It's about infusing your interactions with genuine interest, empathy, and respect. It's about creating a space where connection thrives, ideas are exchanged, and hearts are touched.

So, embark on this journey with an open mind and a curious heart. Experiment, practice, and learn from every interaction. Embrace the stumbles as stepping stones, and celebrate the successes as milestones on your path to becoming a masterful conversationalist. Remember, the most impactful endings are often those that leave a lingering feeling of warmth, connection, and a longing for more.

With every conversation you navigate, you have the potential to spark positive change, inspire others, and leave a lasting mark on the world. Let the art of ending conversations be your guide, and watch as your interactions blossom into powerful tools for building meaningful relationships and creating a more connected and compassionate world.

CHAPTER 17: The Power of Conversation

In the vast tapestry of human experience, conversation stands as a radiant thread, weaving together the intricate strands of connection, understanding, and growth. It serves as the cornerstone of meaningful relationships, the engine driving progress, and the fuel that ignites innovation. It's not merely an exchange of words, but rather a captivating dance of ideas, a journey of discovery, and a gateway to unseen worlds. It acts as a mirror that reflects the perspectives of others, while simultaneously offering a glimpse into our own unexplored depths.

The power of conversation transcends the ordinary; it possesses the potential to:

1) **Forge Deep Connections:** When we engage in truly authentic conversations, we transcend the shallow waters of small talk and delve deep into the core of each other's being. We lay bare our experiences, vulnerabilities, and aspirations, creating a sanctuary for genuine understanding and empathy. This profound connection fosters trust and intimacy, strengthening the invisible threads that bind us together.

2) **Ignite Creativity and Spark Innovation:** Conversation is a fertile ground where new ideas can blossom. By sharing our thoughts and perspectives with others, we stimulate each other's minds and challenge ingrained ways of thinking. This collaborative exchange ignites a fire of creativity, leading to breakthroughs and innovations that would remain dormant in isolation.

3) **Navigate Challenges and Overcome Obstacles:** When faced with life's inevitable hurdles, conversation serves as a powerful tool for problem-solving and conflict resolution. By discussing our challenges with others, we

102

gain valuable alternative perspectives and embark on a shared brainstorming session, seeking potential solutions. This collaborative approach fosters a sense of unity and allows us to navigate around obstacles, ultimately finding common ground and achieving positive outcomes.

4) **Cultivate Understanding and Embrace Tolerance:** Conversation acts as a potent antidote to prejudice and fear. Engaging in open and honest dialogue with individuals from diverse backgrounds enables us to confront our own biases and develop a deeper appreciation for the tapestry of human experience. This cultivates a more inclusive and tolerant society where differences are not just accepted, but celebrated, and respect becomes the cornerstone of our interactions.

5) **Transform Lives:** The impact of a single conversation can have a profound and lasting influence on the trajectory of someone's life. Words of encouragement, a listening ear, or a shared perspective can be the catalyst for personal growth, self-discovery, and positive change. They hold the power to shift perspectives, rekindle hope, and inspire individuals to embark on journeys of self-improvement, leaving a lasting mark on their lives.

Unlocking the Potential:

While the power of conversation is undeniable, harnessing it requires consistent effort and dedicated practice. Here are some key strategies to unlock its transformative potential:

- ✓ **Be Present and Engaged:** Devote your full attention to the person you are conversing with, silencing distractions and multitasking to ensure your complete presence in the moment.

- ✓ **Practice Active Listening:** Not only listen to their words, but also pay close attention to their non-verbal cues, demonstrating genuine interest and understanding through your body language and facial expressions.

- ✓ **Craft Open-Ended Questions:** Encourage deeper conversations by asking questions that go beyond mere "yes" or "no" answers. Instead, delve into the heart of the matter with thought-provoking prompts that invite elaborate responses.

103

- ✓ **Embrace Authenticity and Vulnerability:** Share your own thoughts and feelings openly, creating a safe space for genuine connection and fostering mutual understanding.

- ✓ **Respect Diverse Perspectives:** Remain open to new ideas and differing viewpoints, even if they challenge your own preconceived notions. Embrace the opportunity to learn and grow from diverse perspectives.

- ✓ **Mind Your Non-Verbal Communication:** Utilize eye contact, body language, and tone of voice strategically to convey your message effectively and ensure clear communication.

- ✓ **Practice Regularly:** The more you engage in meaningful conversations, the more confident and skilled you will become. Treat every interaction as an opportunity to hone your communication abilities.

By consciously cultivating the art of conversation, we unlock its transformative power, enriching every facet of our lives. We forge deeper connections, ignite the flames of creativity, navigate challenges with ease, build bridges across differences, and foster a world brimming with understanding and compassion. Remember, every conversation, no matter how small, has the potential to create ripples of change that extend far beyond the immediate exchange. Let us become stewards of this powerful tool, wielding its potential wisely and embracing the transformative power of conversation.

Let us leave the world a little brighter, a little more connected, and a little more understanding, one meaningful conversation at a time.

Examples of the Power of Conversation:

Here are some concrete examples that illustrate the transformative power of conversation:

1) **The Unexpected Connection:** Two strangers, seated next to each other on a long-haul flight, strike up a conversation. Sharing their stories, they discover a shared passion for photography. This chance encounter leads to a lifelong friendship and numerous collaborative projects, enriching their lives in ways they could never have anticipated.

104

2) **The Breakthrough Idea**: A group of scientists, struggling to solve a complex problem, gather for a brainstorming session. Through open and honest conversation, they challenge each other's assumptions and explore new avenues of thought. This collaborative exchange leads to a breakthrough discovery, paving the way for advancements in their field.

3) **The Healing Dialogue**: A parent, concerned about their child's behavior, initiates a conversation. By actively listening and expressing empathy, they create a safe space for their child to open up and share their feelings. This open communication fosters understanding and trust, allowing them to work together towards finding a solution.

4) **The Cultural Bridge**: Two individuals from different cultures engage in a respectful dialogue. By sharing their perspectives and experiences, they gain a deeper appreciation for each other's customs and traditions. This cross-cultural exchange fosters tolerance and understanding, breaking down barriers and building bridges between communities.

5) **The Life-Changing Moment**: A young individual, feeling lost and unsure of their future, seeks advice from a mentor. Through a heartfelt conversation, the mentor offers words of encouragement and shares their own experiences. This act of compassion reignites hope and inspires the young person to pursue their dreams, ultimately leading them on a path of fulfillment and joy.

These are just a few examples of the countless ways that conversation can impact our lives. From forging deep connections to sparking innovation and overcoming challenges, the power of conversation is undeniable. By recognizing its potential and consciously cultivating this essential skill, we can unlock its transformative power and create a more connected, understanding, and vibrant world.

The Ripple Effect:

The impact of a single conversation can extend far beyond the immediate exchange. Like a pebble dropped into a still pond, the ripples of a meaningful conversation can spread outward, creating positive changes in unexpected places.

Imagine a conversation between two friends where they discuss their aspirations to travel the world. Inspired by each other's dreams, they decide to save money and plan a trip together. This shared experience strengthens their bond and creates lasting memories. But the impact goes beyond their friendship. They share their

105

travel stories and photos with others, inspiring them to pursue their own travel dreams. This creates a chain reaction, with each conversation igniting a spark of wanderlust and encouraging others to explore the world.

Similarly, a conversation about overcoming personal challenges can inspire others facing similar struggles. Sharing stories of resilience and perseverance can offer hope and encouragement, empowering individuals to navigate their own difficulties. This ripple effect of positive influence highlights the transformative power of conversation, demonstrating how our words and experiences can impact the lives of others in profound ways.

Conclusion

In a world often characterized by division and noise, conversation emerges as a powerful force for connection, understanding, and positive change. By embracing the art of conversation and harnessing its potential, we can forge deeper bonds, ignite creativity, overcome obstacles, and cultivate a more compassionate and vibrant world. Let us, therefore, become mindful stewards of this powerful tool, engaging in meaningful conversations that leave a lasting legacy of connection and mutual understanding. Let every dialogue be a bridge across differences, a catalyst for innovation, and a testament to the transformative power of human connection.

Remember, the world is waiting to be enriched by your voice. Start a conversation today and witness the magic unfold.

CHAPTER 18: Conversation Skills for Business

The art of conversation becomes even more nuanced and crucial in the dynamic landscape of business. Here, conversations aren't simply social exchanges – they are the very tools that build relationships, forge partnerships, secure deals, and navigate challenges. Mastering conversation skills in this context can elevate your career, unlock doors to new opportunities, and leave a lasting positive impression. Let's delve into the unique dynamics of business conversations and equip you with essential skills to thrive in this arena.

Understanding the Business Context:

1) **Audience:** Unlike casual conversations, which might involve friends or acquaintances with shared interests, business interactions often involve diverse audiences with varying backgrounds, expectations, and industry knowledge. For example, if you're pitching a marketing strategy to a team of investors, your communication style and content will need to be tailored differently than if you were brainstorming ideas with a group of young, tech-savvy colleagues. Understanding your audience's specific needs, expectations, and industry knowledge is crucial for tailoring your communication accordingly.

2) **Objectives:** Every business conversation has a specific purpose, whether it's securing a new client, networking with potential collaborators, or resolving a conflict with a colleague. Clearly identifying your intended outcome guides your approach and ensures you utilize the appropriate conversation style. For instance, if your objective is to gather information for a new project,

107

your questions will be different than if you were seeking to persuade someone to invest in your idea.

3) **Professionalism:** While maintaining a friendly and approachable demeanor is essential, remember to uphold a professional tone and avoid personal anecdotes or topics that could be misconstrued. This doesn't mean you need to become robotic or overly formal, but rather maintain a balance between respectful communication and genuine warmth.

Conversation Strategies for Business:

1) **Preparation is Key:**

   ✓ **Research your audience:** Gather information about their company, industry expertise, and individual roles within the organization. This helps you find common ground and tailor your conversation to their specific interests. For example, if you're meeting with a potential client who is known for their expertise in sustainable marketing practices, you could prepare relevant case studies or research showcasing your company's commitment to environmental responsibility.

   ✓ **Anticipate questions:** Prepare answers to potential inquiries about your company, products, services, or qualifications. Rehearse your responses for key points to ensure you deliver clear and concise information.

   ✓ **Develop talking points:** Have a clear outline of topics you want to discuss, ensuring you stay focused on the main points and cover all relevant information. This prevents rambling or digression and keeps the conversation productive.

2) **Building Rapport and Trust:**

   ✓ Start with a warm greeting and introduce yourself confidently. Projecting positive body language and making eye contact sets the tone for a comfortable and engaging interaction.

   ✓ Actively listen to understand their interests and perspectives. Give them your full attention, ask clarifying questions, and demonstrate genuine interest in what they have to say.

108

✓ **Ask insightful questions that encourage dialogue and demonstrate your curiosity.** Avoid generic questions that can be answered with a simple "yes" or "no." Instead, ask open-ended questions that invite elaboration and offer deeper insights. For example, instead of asking "Are you interested in our marketing campaign?" you could ask, "What are your current marketing goals and challenges, and how do you think our campaign might address them?"

✓ **Find common ground and share relevant experiences to connect on a deeper level.** This could be shared industry knowledge, mutual connections, or even hobbies and interests outside of work. Finding common ground fosters a sense of connection and trust, which is essential for building lasting relationships.

3) **Communication Skills for Business Interactions:**

✓ **Clarity and conciseness:** Avoid jargon and technical terms your audience may not understand. Use plain language, simple sentences, and concrete examples to ensure your message is clear and easy to grasp.

✓ **Directness and assertiveness:** Communicate your message directly and confidently. Avoid being overly apologetic or hesitant, but also avoid coming across as aggressive or domineering. Aim for a balance between clear communication and respectful demeanor.

✓ **Positive body language:** Maintain eye contact, smile, and use open gestures to convey confidence, engagement, and enthusiasm. Avoid fidgeting, crossing your arms, or looking away, as these can send mixed messages and undermine your message.

✓ **Active listening:** Pay close attention to both verbal and nonverbal cues. Acknowledge their points with verbal affirmations, head nods, and engaged expressions to demonstrate you are actively listening and understand their perspective.

✓ **Effective questioning:** Ask open-ended questions that encourage dialogue and gather valuable information. This demonstrates your interest in their perspective and helps you understand their needs and concerns better.

109

✓ **Storytelling:** Share relevant anecdotes, case studies, or client testimonials to illustrate your points and make your message more impactful. Stories are engaging, memorable, and often more persuasive than dry facts and figures.

4) **Handling Difficult Conversations:**

✓ **Stay calm and professional:** Even in challenging situations, it's crucial to maintain composure and avoid getting defensive or emotional. Reacting impulsively can escalate tensions and harm the conversation's progress.

✓ **Listen actively and acknowledge their concerns:** Demonstrate empathy by acknowledging their perspective and validating their feelings. This helps de-escalate the situation and creates a safe space for open communication.

✓ **Focus on finding solutions:** Instead of dwelling on the problem, shift the focus towards finding a mutually beneficial solution. Ask clarifying questions to understand the underlying issue and brainstorm potential solutions collaboratively.

✓ **Communicate your boundaries:** While remaining professional and respectful, be clear about your limitations and what you are not comfortable discussing. Don't hesitate to politely decline unreasonable requests or redirect the conversation back to productive topics.

✓ **Seek support:** If a situation becomes too difficult to manage alone, don't hesitate to seek assistance from a colleague or mediator. A neutral third party can offer objective perspective and help facilitate a productive conversation.

5) **Closing the Conversation:**

✓ **Summarize key points and next steps:** Briefly recap the main takeaways from the conversation and outline any agreed-upon action items. This ensures clarity and prevents misunderstandings.

- ✓ **Express your appreciation for their time and consideration**: Thank them for their time and express your gratitude for their participation in the conversation.

- ✓ **End with a positive and professional note**: Convey a positive outlook and express your enthusiasm for future collaboration or continued interaction.

Additional Tips for Success:

- ✓ **Be mindful of cultural differences**: Adapt your communication style to respect different cultural norms and communication preferences. For example, maintain eye contact when speaking with someone from a culture that values directness, but avoid prolonged eye contact with someone from a culture that considers it disrespectful.

- ✓ **Follow up promptly**: After any business conversation, send a thank-you note or follow-up email to reiterate key points, express your continued interest, and keep the momentum going.

- ✓ **Continuously learn and improve**: Seek feedback from colleagues and mentors on your communication skills and actively practice your conversation abilities in various settings. Attend workshops, join professional organizations, and network with individuals from diverse backgrounds to broaden your perspective and enhance your communication repertoire.

Conclusion

By mastering the art of conversation in a business context, you equip yourself with a powerful tool for success. Remember, effective communication is not just about conveying information; it's about connecting authentically, building trust, and fostering collaboration. Through mindful preparation, active listening, clear communication, and a genuine interest in others, you can transform your business interactions into opportunities for growth, connection, and lasting impact. So, embrace the power of conversation, refine your skills, and watch your career soar to new heights.

111

CHAPTER 19: Conversations for Romance and Relationships

The landscape of conversation shifts dramatically when it comes to romance and relationships. In the realm of love and connection, conversations become the bridge that fosters intimacy, understanding, and a lasting bond. This chapter equips you with the tools and strategies to navigate conversations that strengthen your romantic relationships and pave the way for a deeper connection with your partner.

<u>A Landscape Unlike Any Other:</u>

Conversations in intimate relationships demand a delicate balance. You'll need to cultivate a safe space where both partners feel comfortable sharing their thoughts, feelings, and vulnerabilities. This involves actively listening without judgment, offering unconditional positive regard, and prioritizing empathy over criticism.

Instead of focusing solely on everyday discussions about work, schedules, or chores, aim for deeper conversations that explore each other's values, dreams, fears, and aspirations. These discussions reveal the core of who you are as individuals and as a couple.

Active engagement is key. Be present and put away distractions like phones or laptops. Maintain eye contact, use active listening techniques like nodding and paraphrasing, and be responsive to your partner's emotions. Remember, attentive listening speaks volumes.

<u>Embracing Vulnerability:</u>

112

Vulnerability is the cornerstone of deep connection. Sharing your true self, including insecurities and past experiences, fosters trust and intimacy. This doesn't mean spilling every detail of your life story at once. Start small, share a personal story, and invite your partner to reciprocate.

Honesty and openness are essential for building a strong foundation. Be transparent and honest in your communication, even when dealing with difficult topics. Remember, honesty doesn't mean brutal honesty. Be mindful of your partner's feelings and communicate your thoughts in a respectful and constructive manner.

Conversation Starters for Deepening Connection:

- ✓ **Memory Lane:** Relive special moments you've shared, reminisce about your first date, or talk about what attracted you to each other initially. This rekindles the flame of your initial spark and reminds you why you fell in love.

- ✓ **Dreamweaving:** Discuss your individual and shared dreams for the future. Talk about your career goals, travel aspirations, or your vision for your relationship. This allows you to work towards a common goal and build a shared future together.

- ✓ **Values and Beliefs:** Explore each other's core values, beliefs, and perspectives on life. Understanding your partner's motivations and decision-making processes can bridge the gap between your individual backgrounds and create a sense of acceptance.

- ✓ **Appreciation and Support:** Express your appreciation for your partner, acknowledge their efforts, and offer support when they need it. Words of affirmation and gestures of support go a long way in strengthening your bond and making your partner feel valued and loved.

- ✓ **Unlocking Desires:** Share your deepest desires and fantasies with your partner. This can add a touch of excitement and intimacy to your conversations and explore new depths within your relationship. Remember, open communication is essential in a healthy relationship.

- ✓ **Facing Challenges Together:** Address any challenges or conflicts in your relationship openly and honestly. Bottling up emotions can create distance and resentment. Communicate your needs effectively and work together to

113

find solutions. Remember, conflict resolution is a skill that can be learned and perfected.

- ✓ **Gratitude and Affirmations**: Regularly express your gratitude for each other's presence in your life and offer positive affirmations. This reminds your partner of their value and the positive impact they have on your life.

Beyond Words:

Remember, conversation is not just about words. Pay attention to non-verbal cues like body language, facial expressions, and tone of voice. These nonverbal cues can often reveal unspoken emotions and offer deeper insights into your partner's thoughts and feelings.

Remember:

- ✓ **Consistency is Key**: Cultivating a deeper connection with your partner requires consistent effort, open communication, and a willingness to be vulnerable. It's not a one-time event, but an ongoing process of exploration and growth.

- ✓ **Experiment and Adapt**: Every relationship is unique, and what works for one couple may not work for another. Don't be afraid to experiment with different conversation starters and techniques. Find what resonates with you and your partner and adapt your approach as needed.

- ✓ **Embrace the Journey**: Most importantly, have fun exploring the art of conversation together. Enjoy the process of learning more about each other, building trust, and deepening your connection. As you delve deeper into these conversations, you'll discover a new dimension to your relationship and unlock a level of intimacy you never thought possible.

Remember, these resources are just a starting point. The most important ingredient in any relationship is your commitment to open communication, vulnerability, and a willingness to learn and grow together.

Conversation Starters for Specific Situations:

Here are some additional conversation starters tailored to specific situations:

114

First Date:

- ✓ What are you passionate about?
- ✓ What are your thoughts on love and relationships?
- ✓ What are some of your biggest dreams?
- ✓ What's the most adventurous thing you've ever done?
- ✓ What's your favorite book, movie, or song, and why?

Long-Term Relationship:

- ✓ How can I support you better?
- ✓ What are you grateful for about our relationship?
- ✓ What are some challenges you're facing right now?
- ✓ What are your hopes and dreams for our future together?
- ✓ What can we do to keep the spark alive in our relationship?

Difficult Conversations:

- ✓ How can we resolve this conflict in a way that works for both of us?
- ✓ What are your needs in this situation?
- ✓ What are my needs in this situation?
- ✓ How can we communicate more effectively in the future?
- ✓ What can we do to rebuild trust and intimacy in our relationship?

Remember, there are no perfect conversations. The important thing is to approach your partner with an open heart and a willingness to listen and understand. By making a conscious effort to improve your communication skills, you can build a stronger, more fulfilling relationship with your partner.

<u>**Bonus Tips:**</u>

- ✓ **Create a regular time for uninterrupted conversation:** This could be a weekly check-in, a dedicated date night, or simply setting aside 15 minutes each day to talk without distractions.

- ✓ **Be mindful of your body language:** Maintain eye contact, use open body language, and avoid crossing your arms or fidgeting.

- ✓ **Be present and engaged in the conversation:** Put away your phone, turn off the TV, and focus on your partner.

- ✓ **Be patient and understanding:** It takes time to build trust and intimacy. Don't expect to have deep, meaningful conversations overnight.

- ✓ **Most importantly, have fun!** Enjoy the process of getting to know your partner better and deepening your connection.

By incorporating these tips and strategies into your conversations, you can create a lasting bond with your partner and build a relationship that is filled with love, understanding, and joy.

Conclusion

The art of conversation takes on a powerful and intimate form when applied to romance and relationships. By fostering open communication, embracing vulnerability, and actively engaging with your partner, you can cultivate a deep connection that transcends the everyday. Remember, it's a journey, not a destination. Explore different approaches, experiment with conversation starters, and most importantly, have fun along the way. As you delve deeper into meaningful conversations, you'll not only unlock a new level of intimacy but also build a relationship that thrives on understanding, love, and shared dreams.

CHAPTER 20: Conversations for Life

Conversation is the lifeblood of human connection. It's the bridge between hearts, the tapestry of shared experiences, and the fuel that propels us through life's joys and challenges. In this final chapter, we embark on a journey through the vibrant landscape of conversations across various stages of our lives, equipping you with valuable insights and strategies to cultivate meaningful connections throughout your unique path.

1) **Conversations Across the Spectrum of Life:**

   ✓ **Childhood:** Our earliest interactions lay the foundation for future communication patterns. Imagine a nurturing home where curiosity is encouraged and open dialogue flourishes. Parents who actively listen to their children's stories and engage in imaginative play foster a sense of security, trust, and self-expression. These early interactions become the building blocks for forming healthy relationships and navigating the complexities of life.

   ✓ **Adolescence:** As we enter the turbulent waters of adolescence, friends become our confidants and allies. Conversations shift towards identity, self-discovery, and navigating the social landscape. Open communication with trusted adults, whether parents, teachers, or mentors, provides crucial support and guidance during this formative period. Sharing anxieties, exploring dreams, and receiving constructive feedback empower teenagers to make informed choices and build resilience during this transformative time.

   ✓ **Adulthood:** Conversations in adulthood become multifaceted, encompassing professional settings, romantic relationships, and the

117

intricate web of friendships. Mastering the art of articulate communication becomes a vital tool for building strong partnerships, fostering collaboration, and achieving professional goals. Imagine a job interview where your confidence shines through as you engage in a captivating dialogue with the interviewer, sharing your experiences and demonstrating your passion for the role. Conversely, picture a heated conversation with your partner, where active listening and empathy pave the way for understanding and resolution. As we navigate the complexities of adult life, the ability to communicate effectively becomes increasingly crucial for establishing fulfilling relationships and achieving personal fulfillment.

✓ **Later Life**: As we age, conversations take on a new dimension. Sharing stories of our youth, reminiscing about cherished memories, and engaging in meaningful dialogue with loved ones can combat feelings of isolation and provide a sense of purpose. Imagine a group of elderly friends gathered around a table, sharing stories and laughter, their faces aglow with the warmth of shared experiences. In later life, conversations offer a powerful tool for maintaining social connections, combating loneliness, and enriching our golden years.

2) **Conversations Tailored to Specific Situations:**

✓ **Job Interviews**: Landing your dream job often hinges on your ability to articulate your skills and experiences effectively. Imagine a well-prepared interview where you confidently answer questions, ask insightful inquiries, and demonstrate genuine enthusiasm for the opportunity. This requires deliberate preparation, practicing your introduction, crafting thoughtful questions, and actively listening to the interviewer's inquiries. By mastering the art of conversation in professional settings, you can significantly increase your chances of securing your desired position.

✓ **Difficult Conversations**: Addressing sensitive topics like conflict or disagreement requires careful navigation. Imagine a tense situation where you practice active listening, utilize "I" statements to express your perspective without blame, and strive to find common ground. This creates a safe space for productive dialogue, facilitating understanding and resolution without resorting to destructive conflict. By equipping yourself with the tools for navigating difficult conversations, you can foster healthier relationships and resolve challenges constructively.

118

- ✓ **Networking Events**: Building a strong professional network often hinges on your ability to engage in meaningful conversations. Picture yourself at a networking event, confidently introducing yourself to others, asking engaging questions, and actively listening to their stories. By demonstrating genuine interest and showcasing your communication skills, you can forge new connections, expand your network, and open doors to exciting opportunities.

3) **Nurturing Connection Through Everyday Conversations:**

- ✓ **Regular Check-ins**: Fostering a sense of connection doesn't require grand gestures. Imagine scheduling regular phone calls or video chats with loved ones, even for brief updates. This simple act of maintaining communication demonstrates care and strengthens the bond, regardless of physical distance.

- ✓ **Active Listening**: Truly listening to others, without interrupting or judging, conveys genuine interest and understanding. Picture yourself giving someone your full attention, making eye contact, and offering encouraging nods. This deepens the connection and creates a safe space for open communication.

- ✓ **Sharing and Vulnerability**: Openly sharing your thoughts, feelings, and experiences requires courage and vulnerability. However, this act of transparency strengthens trust and fosters deeper connections within relationships. Imagine confiding in a close friend, sharing your joys and struggles, and receiving their unwavering support. Such vulnerability paves the way for genuine intimacy and strengthens the bonds of friendship.

- ✓ **Non-Verbal Communication**: Communication extends beyond the spoken word. Imagine yourself maintaining eye contact and utilizing open body language while conversing. These subtle nonverbal cues convey warmth, interest, and attentiveness, amplifying the impact of your message and fostering a more positive and engaging interaction.

4) **A Continuous Journey of Learning and Growth:**

The art of conversation is not a static destination, but rather a dynamic journey of continuous learning and refinement. Just as a sculptor never stops

119

honing their craft, so too must we cultivate our communication skills through deliberate practice and self-reflection. Embrace opportunities to engage in conversation with diverse individuals, seeking feedback from trusted friends and mentors. Explore resources such as books, workshops, and online communities dedicated to communication and interpersonal skills. As you delve deeper into the world of effective communication, you'll discover a plethora of tools and strategies to enhance your ability to connect with others and navigate the intricate tapestry of human relationships.

5) **The Legacy of Conversation:**

Conversations leave behind a lasting legacy, shaping the course of our lives and the lives of those we encounter. Imagine the profound impact of a heartfelt conversation with a loved one, where words of encouragement and support pave the way for their success. Picture the ripple effect of a passionate conversation about a cause you believe in, inspiring others to join your mission and make a positive difference in the world. Through our conversations, we share our wisdom, offer guidance, and contribute to the collective tapestry of knowledge and understanding. By consciously cultivating the art of conversation, we can leave behind a legacy of connection, inspiration, and positive transformation.

Remember:

- ✓ Conversation is a dynamic and ever-evolving process.
- ✓ Each conversation offers a unique opportunity for growth and connection.
- ✓ Be mindful of your communication style and its impact on others.
- ✓ Actively listen, share openly, and be present in the moment.
- ✓ Embrace the transformative power of meaningful conversations throughout your journey.

As we embark on the journey of life, let us remember the profound power of conversation. With each heartfelt dialogue, each insightful question, and each act of genuine listening, we weave a tapestry of connection that enriches our lives and leaves a lasting impact on the world around us. Let us move forward with the intention of fostering meaningful conversations, cultivating deep connections, and leaving behind a legacy that inspires and empowers future generations.

<u>Beyond the Words: Expanding the Art of Conversation</u>

120

While mastering the art of verbal communication is crucial, true connection transcends words alone. The realm of conversation extends beyond language, encompassing the subtle nuances of non-verbal cues, the power of shared experiences, and the magic of silence.

1) **The Language of Non-Verbal Cues:**

   Our bodies speak volumes, even when our lips are sealed. Maintaining eye contact, using open body language, and mirroring the other person's gestures can convey warmth, attentiveness, and genuine interest. Imagine a conversation where you lean in to listen, nod your head with understanding, and offer a reassuring smile. These subtle cues build trust, encourage further communication, and deepen the connection between you and the other person.

2) **Building Shared Experiences:**

   Conversations are not mere exchanges of information; they are opportunities to create shared experiences that strengthen bonds and forge lasting memories. Picture yourself engaging in a lively discussion about a movie you both enjoyed, reliving the highlights with laughter and excitement. This shared experience weaves a thread of connection, creating a unique bond that transcends the words spoken.

3) **The Power of Silence:**

   Silence, often misconstrued as awkwardness, can be a powerful tool in conversation. Imagine a moment in a heartfelt conversation where words fail to express the depth of emotion. A comfortable silence allows for reflection, deepens understanding, and creates a space for unspoken emotions to resonate. By embracing the power of silence, we pave the way for a more profound and meaningful connection.

4) **Embracing Diversity and Connection:**

   Conversations are not confined to familiar faces or shared backgrounds. Engaging in dialogue with individuals from diverse cultures and perspectives opens doors to new worlds of understanding and appreciation. Imagine a conversation with someone from a different country, where you learn about their customs, traditions, and unique perspective on life. This exchange

121

fosters empathy, broadens your worldview, and enriches your own understanding of the human experience.

5) **Cultivating a Conversational Mindset:**

The art of conversation begins with a shift in perspective. It's not simply about "getting your point across," but rather about creating a space for authentic connection and mutual understanding. Approach each conversation with curiosity, openness, and a genuine desire to learn from the other person. Imagine entering a conversation without preconceived notions, eager to listen without judgment and share your own experiences with humility. This shift in mindset fosters genuine connection and transforms conversations into enriching experiences.

6) **Leaving a Legacy Through Conversation:**

The impact of our conversations extends far beyond the immediate moment. The words we share, the stories we tell, and the connections we forge have the power to inspire, empower, and shape the lives of others. Imagine a conversation where you share your dreams and aspirations with a younger person, sparking their own passions and igniting their potential. This legacy of inspiration lives on, impacting future generations and creating a ripple effect of positive change.

As you navigate the intricate dance of conversation, remember:

- ✓ Words are just one tool in the vast toolbox of communication.
- ✓ Embrace the power of non-verbal cues, shared experiences, and even silence.
- ✓ Seek out opportunities to connect with individuals from diverse backgrounds.
- ✓ Cultivate a conversational mindset of curiosity, openness, and genuine interest.
- ✓ Recognize the profound impact your conversations can have on others.

By weaving these threads together, we can transform the art of conversation into a tapestry of connection, leaving a lasting legacy that enriches our lives and inspires generations to come. Remember, every conversation is an opportunity to connect, grow, and leave a positive mark on the world. Let us use this gift of communication wisely and build a future filled with meaningful connections and transformative dialogue.

Beyond the Everyday: Conversations for Change:

The power of conversation extends beyond personal connections, offering a potent instrument for positive change. By harnessing the collective voice and shared experiences of individuals, conversations can spark social movements, advocate for justice, and pave the way for a more just and equitable world.

1) **Conversations for Social Change:**

   Imagine a group of passionate individuals engaging in open dialogue about a social injustice they witness. As they share their experiences and perspectives, a collective voice emerges, demanding change and inspiring action. This type of conversation can be the catalyst for social movements, mobilizing communities and drawing attention to crucial issues.

2) **Conversations for Advocacy:**

   Advocacy often hinges on the ability to communicate effectively and generate empathy. Picture yourself advocating for a cause you believe in, using your words to paint a vivid picture of the issue's impact and inspire others to join your cause. By crafting compelling narratives and engaging in open dialogue with policymakers and the public, you can effectively advocate for change and drive progress towards a better future.

3) **Conversations for Healing and Reconciliation:**

   Open and honest dialogue can be a powerful tool for healing past wounds and fostering reconciliation. Imagine a community dialogue after a period of conflict, where individuals from diverse backgrounds share their stories of pain and loss. This act of listening and acknowledging shared experiences creates a space for healing and forgiveness, laying the foundation for a more just and peaceful future.

4) **Conversations for Innovation and Problem-Solving:**

   Collaboration and the exchange of ideas are essential for innovation and problem-solving. Imagine a brainstorming session where diverse perspectives are welcomed and encouraged. As individuals share their unique

123

ideas and engage in open discussion, innovative solutions and creative approaches to complex challenges emerge. This type of collaborative conversation fosters a culture of innovation and empowers individuals to contribute to solving the world's most pressing problems.

5) **Conversations for Global Understanding:**

In our increasingly interconnected world, cross-cultural dialogue is crucial for building bridges and promoting global understanding. Imagine a conversation between individuals from different countries, where they share their cultural perspectives and seek to learn from each other's experiences. This open exchange of ideas fosters empathy, breaks down stereotypes, and paves the way for cooperation and collaboration on a global scale.

As we navigate the complex landscape of social change:

- ✓ Remember the power of collective voices and shared stories.
- ✓ Use your words to advocate for justice and inspire action.
- ✓ Embrace dialogue and open communication as tools for healing and reconciliation.
- ✓ Foster collaboration and exchange of ideas to spark innovation and problem-solving.
- ✓ Build bridges of understanding through cross-cultural conversations.

By harnessing the transformative power of conversation, we can become agents of positive change, working together to create a world filled with justice, equality, and understanding. Let us use our voices to speak out for what we believe in, engage in meaningful dialogue with others, and leave behind a legacy of positive change that resonates across generations.

Conclusion

As we close this final chapter, we stand at the precipice of a boundless journey. The art of conversation is not a destination, but a continuous tapestry woven with the threads of our experiences, interactions, and shared humanity. With each heartfelt dialogue, each insightful question, and each act of genuine listening, we add a new layer to our personal tapestry, strengthening the bonds of connection and leaving a lasting imprint on the world around us.

124

Throughout this exploration, we've journeyed through the diverse landscapes of conversation – from childhood whispers to the wisdom of later years, from intimate moments to the vibrant forum of social change. We've delved into the nuances of active listening, the power of non-verbal communication, and the transformative potential of silence. And through it all, we've discovered that the true art of conversation lies not in mere words, but in the genuine human connection that unfolds within the space we create for one another.

As we move forward, let us carry these insights like precious jewels, adorning our communication with empathy, respect, and a genuine desire to connect. Let us actively seek out diverse perspectives, embracing the richness of human experience and learning from each encounter. Let us remember the profound impact our conversations can have, fostering understanding, inspiring action, and leaving behind a legacy that resonates with generations to come.

For the art of conversation is more than simply exchanging words; it is the very fabric of human connection, the bridge between hearts, and the lifeblood of a shared journey. May we continue to weave this tapestry with intention, care, and a spirit of wonder, forever seeking to deepen our understanding of ourselves and the world around us.

And so, with a heart full of gratitude and a mind brimming with possibilities, we embark on the next chapter of our conversation – the grand conversation of life itself.

CONCLUSION

Throughout this book, we've embarked on a journey together, exploring the intricacies and nuances of the art of conversation. We've delved into the depths of self-discovery, honing our listening skills, and mastering the art of asking questions. We've learned to communicate with empathy and understanding, building rapport and trust through the power of authentic connection. We've explored strategies for overcoming shyness and social anxiety, and discovered the secrets to starting conversations with confidence and keeping them flowing effortlessly. We've navigated the art of storytelling, tackled difficult topics with grace, and learned to handle silences and awkward moments with poise. We've witnessed the transformative power of conversation, its ability to build bridges, strengthen relationships, and foster a more connected world.

As we conclude this exploration, remember that the art of conversation is a lifelong pursuit. It requires constant learning, practice, and self-reflection. There will be moments of awkwardness, stumbles along the way, and conversations that don't quite unfold as planned. But through it all, hold onto the joy of human connection, the thrill of shared experiences, and the magic that unfolds when two souls truly meet in conversation.

Here are some final takeaways to guide you on your journey:

- ✓ **Embrace the power of vulnerability**: Authentic connections are built on vulnerability. Sharing your true thoughts, feelings, and experiences invites others to do the same, creating a deeper level of understanding and intimacy.

- ✓ **Never underestimate the power of listening**: When you truly listen with an open mind and heart, you gain invaluable insights and perspectives. You build trust and create a safe space for others to express themselves freely.

126

✓ **Ask questions that spark curiosity and ignite conversation:** The right question can unlock a hidden world of thoughts and experiences. By asking open-ended questions, you encourage deeper reflection and meaningful dialogue.

✓ **Practice empathy and compassion:** Put yourself in the other person's shoes and try to see the world through their eyes. This fosters a sense of connection and understanding, allowing you to build genuine relationships.

✓ **Embrace the beauty of silence:** Not every moment requires words. Sometimes, the most profound communication happens in the space between words, where hearts and souls resonate in unspoken understanding.

✓ **Never stop learning and growing:** The art of conversation is a constant journey of discovery. Embrace opportunities to learn from others, read books on communication, and practice your skills in everyday interactions.

✓ **Remember, conversation is a gift:** It is a chance to connect, to learn, to grow, and to experience the richness of human connection. Choose your words wisely, speak from the heart, and embrace the joy of authentic communication.

As you embark on your own conversational adventures, may you carry with you the lessons learned and the tools acquired. May your conversations be filled with laughter, understanding, and the profound joy of human connection. Go forth and converse with confidence, knowing that you have the power to make a difference in the world, one meaningful conversation at a time.